YALE STUDIES IN

ALBERT S. COOK, I

LX

THE MEDIÆVAL ATTITUDE TOWARD ASTROLOGY

PARTICULARLY IN ENGLAND

BY

THEODORE OTTO WEDEL

Instructor in English in Yale University

A Dissertation presented to the Faculty of the Graduate School
of Yale University in Candidacy for the Degree of
Doctor of Philosophy

NEW HAVEN: YALE UNIVERSITY PRESS
LONDON: HUMPHREY MILFORD
OXFORD UNIVERSITY PRESS

MDCCCCXX

PREFACE

Mediæval astrology has long suffered a neglect which, judged intrinsically, it deserves. Little more than a romantic interest now attaches to a complex divinatory art that for centuries has been looked upon as one of the aberrations of the human mind. When viewed historically, however, astrology is seen to have occupied a place in art and philosophy which many a later science might envy, and which, consequently, it is not well to ignore. Ancient astrology, indeed, has already received in recent years close and appreciative study. The poem of Manilius has never lost its appeal for the classicist; and the prominence of astrological thought in ancient philosophy and ethics has frequently aroused the curiosity of scholars. A history of mediæval astrology, on the other hand, still remains to be written.

Yet for the men of the thirteenth century, even more than for the poets and philosophers of Greece and Rome, the rule of the stars over human destinies was an indisputable fact, entering into their every conception of the universe. In that sudden revival of Aristotelian and Arabian learning which, in the twelfth century, heralded the scholastic age, astrology was hailed as the chief of the sciences. Although a long warfare with theology had to precede its acceptance by mediæval orthodoxy, its final triumph was complete. Theologians dared to credit the stars with a power second only to that of God himself. When Chaucer, in lines echoing Dante's *Inferno,* exclaims

> O influences of thise hevenes hye!
> Soth is, that, under God, ye ben our hierdes,

he is expressing the conviction of the best mediæval thinkers. Astrology, offering, as it did, a reasoned explanation of an infinite diversity of physical phenomena, and including in its scope psychology and ethics, made possible even in the Middle Ages dreams of a universal science.

I have endeavored in this dissertation to trace the development of mediæval thought concerning astrology from Augustine to the fifteenth century, and to interpret references to it in mediæval English literature. The larger purpose was a direct outgrowth of the second—a summary of astrological passages in Old and Middle English proving barren without an interpretative background. It will be easily recognized that the treatment of mediæval astrology as a whole is cursory and incomplete. A field so little explored as that of Arabian and Jewish science offers countless difficulties to the novice. But the general trend of astrological opinion in the Middle Ages seemed not impossible of discovery, and called for at least a tentative explanation.

The recent investigations of several scholars have encouraged my interest in the present work. Professor Tatlock's studies on the astrology of Chaucer were responsible for my first intelligent view of the problem. Some twenty pages of incidental exposition in his *Scene of the Franklin's Tale Visited* constitute the most suggestive monograph of mediæval astrology with which I am acquainted. The earlier volumes of Duhem's *Système du Monde* also aided me in matters bibliographical, and in outlining the evolution of scientific ideas from Aristotle to modern times. Although my introductory discussion of ancient astrology is based upon Bouché-Leclercq's *Astrologie Grecque,* I have endeavored to interpret the early history of the science in the light of its later development. The principal contribution of the present study, in fact, will be found to consist in an attempt to explain the mediæval attitude toward astrology as the result of a combat between an ecclesiastical hostility, inherited from the ancient Church, and the increasingly insistent demands of Arabian science.

My thanks are due to the officials of the Library of Yale University, who secured for me many of the books here cited; to Professor J. S. P. Tatlock, of Leland Stanford University, and Professor T. F. Crane, of Cornell University, for courteous replies to queries; and to Professor C. C. Torrey and Professor Williston Walker, of Yale University, for aid in solving problems of Oriental bibliography. My gratitude to Professor Albert Stanburrough Cook, under whom this dissertation was written, must be left largely unexpressed. Professor Cook helped me everywhere, always ungrudging of his time, and always ready with sympathetic counsel.

A portion of the expense of printing this thesis has been borne by the Modern Language Club of Yale University, from funds placed at its disposal by the generosity of the late Mr. George E. Dimock, a graduate of Yale in the Class of 1874.

YALE UNIVERSITY,
November, 1919.

CONTENTS

CHAPTER I

ANCIENT ASTROLOGY

I

Little is definitely known of the history of astrology before its advent in the Greek world at the time of the Alexandrian empire. Arising somewhere in the Chaldean East, and spreading early over Egypt, it won its first foothold in the West in a school of astrologers founded by Berosus on the island of Cos. Astrological divination among the Babylonians seems to have been of a primitive sort, confining itself to eclipses, and to general prophecies concerning kings and realms. It was in the hands of the Greeks that astrology developed into that intricate science of divination, fortified by the best philosophical thought of the time, which we encounter in the classic texts of Manilius and Ptolemy.[1]

Though astrology entered the Greek world late, it found a soil prepared for its reception. Popular superstitions regarding lucky and unlucky days have been current among all peoples; Hesiod had sung of them in his *Works and Days*. Astrology, furthermore, won ready converts among the philosophers. Though the contemporaneous Stoic school was the first openly to espouse its doctrines, astrology discovered many points of contact in the systems that had preceded. Pythagoreanism, with its mystic numbers, seemed expressly made for the new science. The four elements of Empedocles found here a new home. And of the utmost importance for its later history were the relations which astrology formed with the philosophical systems of Plato

[1] The authoritative study of Greek astrology is Bouché-Leclercq's *L'Astrologie Grecque*, Paris, 1899. Chaldean astrology is discussed on pp. 35-72. The best short account of ancient astrology is the article *Astrologie* by E. Riess, in Pauly-Wissowa's *Real-encyclopädie der Classischen Alterthumswissenschaft* (Stuttgart, 1896) 1. 1802-28.

and Aristotle.   With Platonism, astrology experienced little
difficulty.   The *Timæus* became in later times a veritable
breviary, not only for astrologers, but for teachers of magic
of all sorts.   The myth of the Demiurge, creating the world
as a living organism, every part of which was intimately
related to every other, presented the very principle that with
the Stoics became the corner-stone of the ancient faith in
divination.   Man, as a microcosm, the Stoics said, merely
reflected the great world about and above him.   Moreover,
the picture in the *Timæus* of the soul descending from the
upper heavens by way of the planetary gods, each endowing
it with its proper gifts, was admirably fitted for astrological
interpretation at the hand of the commentator.[1]   To be sure,
when astrology later allied itself with astronomy, and took
on a more scientific aspect, Platonism, with its myths, was
found less adaptable.   So simple an astrological doctrine as
that concerning the evil influence of the planet Saturn
baffled the philosophers.   How could a beneficent planetary
god be the source of evil?   The Neoplatonist, Plotinus,
solved such difficulties by saying that the stars were not
causes of anything, but signs only.   This easy explanation
became general among Platonists.   It is found as late as
the scholastic, William of Auvergne, and the Renaissance
philosopher, Marsilio Ficino.

While astrology discovered a ready ally in Plato, it found
only an indifferent one in Aristotle.   To those familiar with

[1] Bouché-Leclercq, pp. 9-25.   The commentaries on the *Timæus*
by the Neoplatonists, Porphyry and Proclus, contain much astrological matter.   By way of Chalcidius and Macrobius (see below,
p. 26), these astrological explanations of the *Timæus* became accessible to the early Middle Ages.   The mediæval popularity of the
Timæus itself is well known.   The Platonic myth of the descent
of the soul, together with its astrological interpretation, found its
way, in the twelfth century, into the *De Mundi Universitate* of
Bernard Silvestris.   Chaucer drew upon this work for a stanza
in the *Man of Law's Tale* (99-106).   See below, pp. 33-5, 146.

mediæval astrology, this seems strange indeed. In the scholastic writers of the thirteenth century, the cosmology of Aristotle furnished the very axioms of the science; it was the authority of Aristotle, more than anything else, that caused its theoretical acceptance by the Church. Thus Aristotle's theory of the fifth essence, teaching that the substance of the stars was of a nobler order than that of the sublunary sphere, was found admirably fitted to form the basis of a science ascribing to the stars the arbitrament over human destinies. This view also found support in Aristotle's physics of motion. All the transformations undergone by physical bodies here on earth, it taught, trace their origin to the local motion of the imperishable beings which constitute the fixed stars. It is this motion, received by the heavens from the Prime Mover himself, and transmitted to the lower spheres, that causes all earthly growth and change. 'The earth,' says Aristotle,[1] 'is bound up in some necessary way with the local motions of the heavens, so that all power that resides in this world is governed by that above.' And in the *locus classicus* for mediæval astrology—the tenth chapter of the second book of the *De Generatione et Corruptione*—Aristotle develops this theory even further. The motion of the heavens, to which all change on earth is due, is twofold, and has a twofold effect on sublunary matter. The perfect diurnal motion of the fixed stars from east to west constitutes the principle of permanence and growth; whereas the motion of the planets, running their annual courses at irregular paces from west to east, athwart the diurnal motion of the fixed stars, constitutes the principle of earthly change. When once interpreted astrologically, Aristotle's physics of motion was all that was needed to fasten upon the Middle Ages that exaggerated belief in the importance of the stars which lay at the basis of the faith in astrology.

[1] *Meteorologica* I. 2.

There are signs that even in the ancient world the possibilities of the Aristotelian cosmology as a fundamental postulate for an astrological science had begun to be recognized. The Peripatetics, Alexander Aphrodisias and Adrastus, based upon it their faith in stellar influence; and when Claudius Ptolemy, in the second century of our era, gave to astrology its final definition as a science, he employed several Aristotelian doctrines. It was Aristotle who had formulated the theory of the four elements—the hot, the cold, the dry, and the moist—which constituted the basis of Ptolemy's physics. By placing these four qualities under the sway of the various planets and constellations, Ptolemy could explain scientifically the manifestations of stellar influence. From the Peripatetics, too, Ptolemy borrowed his masterly solution of the problem of scientific determinism, which, as we shall find, disarmed many critics. Ptolemy, approaching astrology from the side of astronomy, and not from that of mysticism and religion, could in general claim kinship with the spirit of Aristotelian science. But one looks in vain in Ptolemy's proof of the existence of stellar influence[1] for a mention of Aristotle's theory of motion. He speaks on the subject with no such dogmatic sureness as did the scholastic writers twelve centuries later.[2]

Ptolemy, however, comes at the close, not at the begin-

---

[1] *Tetrabiblos* I. 2.

[2] Astrology and early Aristotelianism are discussd by Boll, in *Studien über Claudius Ptolemäus*, pp. 156-162 (*Jahrbücher für Philologie und Pädagogik*, Supplement 21). For Ptolemy's debt to the Peripatetics, see Boll, p. 161, and Bouché-Leclercq, pp. 26-7. Bouché-Leclercq takes Boll to task for the statement that Aristotelianism was in itself favorable to astrology. Platonism, he says, was much more so. From the point of view of ancient astrology, Bouché-Leclercq is probably right. But the history of mediæval astrology proves, I think, that the alliance of astrology with Aristotelianism was the more permanent. It discarded the astrological mythology of Plato, and substituted for it a rational explanation of the universe which captivated the best scientific minds down to

ning, of the history of Greek astrology. In the earlier centuries, no necessity manifested itself of basing astrology upon a scientific conception of the universe. Astrology looked for its first support, not to science, but to philosophy and to religion; and the Chaldean diviner found his first friends, not among the astronomers, but the soothsayers and oracle-mongers. Ptolemy was the first astronomer of note to pay serious attention to astrology. To the Stoics— the one philosophical school that became its staunch ally— astrology was merely a form of divination, accepted and defended along with augury and oracles. In that long controversy of the schools on the subject of divination which is preserved in such writings as Cicero's *De Divinatione*, little mention is made of cosmological principles. The physical influence of the stars, it is true, played a part in the argument. Cicero tried to deny the stars the power to influence human life by saying that all celestial bodies above the sun and moon were too distant.[1] Astrology made answer that the sun and moon were distant, too; yet their influence was manifest. The power of their rays differed only in degree from that exerted by the other heavenly bodies. Ptolemy, preserving for us the arguments of Posidonius, the most important Stoic defender of astrology, points to the influence of the moon upon the ocean, and that of the sun upon the seasons, and then leaves the matter with the assertion that the other heavenly bodies act in a similar manner.[2] Some influence of the stars upon human life was usually taken for granted, and the war was fought out on other issues. The central principle with the Stoics was that of the solidarity of the universe, the resem-

the time of Kepler and Tycho Brahe. The influence of the Aristotelian cosmology upon the later centuries is clearly traced in P. Duhem's *Le Système du Monde: Histoire des Doctrines Cosmologiques de Platon à Copernic* (5 vols., Paris, 1913-7); see especially 1. 164; 2. 277, 300, 334, 368 ff., 389; 3. 248, 342, 351.

[1] *De Divinatione* 2. 43.
[2] *Tetrabiblos* 1. 2.

blance of the part to the whole, the unity of microcosm and macrocosm. With this principle they could defend, not only astrology, but likewise augury from the flight of birds and the entrails of animals, and the various kinds of omens which played so large a part in the superstitious beliefs of the ancients.

The defense of astrology by the Stoics, therefore, concerned itself, not so much with astrology, the science, as with astrology, the art. Their chief opponent on the subject of divination appeared in the person of Carneades (219-126 B. C.), a member of the New Academy. Carneades launched against astrology a series of arguments which remained standard for centuries. These were repeated again and again by the Sceptics, were taken over almost bodily by the Church, and reappear unchanged in Petrarch and Pico della Mirandola. The attack, clever though it was, can not be termed wholly successful, and the followers of Carneades were slow to fashion new weapons. An able defender of astrology appeared with the Stoic, Posidonius (135-50 B. C.) ; and when Ptolemy had finally undertaken its justification in the sane and moderate opening chapters of the *Tetrabiblos,* very few of the arguments of Carneades remained unanswered. Philosophers and theologians of the opposing school, however, content with the brilliant dialectic of Carneades, remained oblivious of these new developments. The work of Carneades himself is no longer extant, but his attack on astrology has been preserved by many later writers—in the second book of Cicero's *De Divinatione,* in the fifth book of Augustine's *De Civitate Dei* (based upon a lost portion of Cicero's *De Fato*), in the writings of the late Sceptic philosopher, Sextus Empiricus, and in the excerpts from the rhetorician Favorinus found in the *Noctes Ambrosianæ* of Aulus Gellius.[1]

[1] For the attitude of Stoicism to astrology, see Bouché-Leclercq, pp. 29-34, 593 ff. The Stoic defense of divination, as a whole, is

The opponents of the Stoics were concerned above all with combating astrological fatalism. Their weapons were plain assertion and the dictates of common sense. They even went far in admitting a rule of the stars over externals, so long as the inner citadel of man's free will remained inviolate. Favorinus declares it intolerable that any one should dare to impute to the heavens the power to intervene in the acts of our own free choice, and to transform man from a reasoning being into a marionette. Closely allied to the argument that astrology was unethical, was the one that it was useless as well. 'If,' says Sextus Empiricus, 'human events are ruled by three things—necessity, chance, and free will—it is useless to foresee what must necessarily happen anyway, and impossible to foresee what is dependent upon chance and the will of man.'[1] But to assert the uselessness and the impiety of astrology was not to discredit it as a science. The Stoics, in fact, faced astrological fatalism without flinching, and dismissed in short order the contention that astrology was useless. According to Posidonius—whose argument is preserved in the third chapter of Ptolemy's *Tetrabiblos*—prophecy is naturally welcome when the thing foreseen is pleasurable; when, on the other hand, the thing foreseen is painful, its prediction prepares the soul to bear misfortune with equanimity.[2]

discussed in the same author's *Histoire de la Divination* (1. 59 ff.). A study of the controversy between the Stoics and the New Academy on the subject of divination has been made by A. Schmekel, in *Die Philosophie der Mittleren Stoa* (Berlin, 1892). Sextus Empiricus, Favorinus, and Cicero, and their joint dependence on Carneades, are discussed on pp. 321-3. Ptolemy's dependence on the Stoic school, and on Posidonius in particular, has been proved by Boll (*op. cit.*, pp. 131 ff.).

[1] Bouché-Leclercq, p. 596; Schmekel, pp. 156, 159.

[2] 'Sed prævisio futurorum animum componit et moderatur meditatione absentium tanquam præsentium, et præparat ad excipienda ventura cum tranquilitate et constantia' (*Tetrabiblos* 1. 3: *Claudii Ptolemæi Omnia quæ extant Opera*, Basel, 1551, p. 381).

Ptolemy himself adds another argument to the one just quoted, in which the utility of astrology is even better defended. Only the movements of the stars themselves, he says, are under the rule of necessity. Happenings on the earth are variable, and subject to other influences, in addition to those exerted by the heavens. A great physical catastrophe, such as a flood or an earthquake, may upset the predictions of a thousand horoscopes. Ptolemy draws a parallel between the astrologer and the physician. The latter may in certain cases be assured that a disease is incurable; in others he may admit the possibility of improvement, if medicines are applied in time. The magnet furnishes another illustration. The law that a magnet always attracts iron is universally accepted; but it is none the less true that if the magnet be rubbed with a piece of garlic, it will refuse to work. Ptolemy argues, to be sure, that if the science were perfect, and if all factors involved in human affairs were known, a predicted destiny would be inescapable. In more general prophecies, indeed, such certainty is already attainable. No one supposes that a prediction of the approach of summer or winter admits of modification. But this does not prevent men, even at the coming of cold weather, from preparing to mitigate its rigors. And if such general predictions are so eminently useful, why should not minute predictions be equally welcome? Does the countryman or the sailor disdain to regulate his daily tasks according to the phases of the moon?[1]

---

[1] *Claudii Ptolemæi Opera*, pp. 381-2. A short outline of the astrological system of Ptolemy will serve as a convenient key to the technical terms used in the following pages. Astrology is divided by Ptolemy into two main parts: 1. That which deals with general predictions (τὸ καθολικόν) regarding war, pestilence, earthquakes, floods, storms, hot and cold weather, and fertility; 2. That which deals with predictions regarding the individual (τὸ γενεθλιαλογικόν), his parents, brothers, length of life, health, riches, profession, marriage, children, and friends. For the purpose of

While, with respect to its philosophical principles, astrology placed itself in an increasingly impregnable position,

general prognostications, the earth was divided into seven 'climates,' each of which was governed by its particular constellations and planets. Thus the advent of an eclipse or a comet could be said to forebode evil for this or that country, according to the constellation in which it first appeared. Ptolemy asserted that the system of general predictions was the surest part of his science. In practice, however, its importance was far less than that which undertook prophecy regarding the fate of the individual. For this genethlialogical astrology, the planets were divided into good (Jupiter and Venus) and bad (Saturn and Mars), while Mercury varied his nature as he stood near a good or a bad neighbor. Some planets ruled over the day (Sun, Saturn, Jupiter), others over the night (Moon, Mars, Venus); some were classed as masculine (Saturn, Jupiter, Mars, Sun), others as feminine (Moon, Venus). Mercury was variable in each case. The signs of the zodiac were divided into masculine and feminine (alternately beginning with the masculine Aries). Constellations and planets were also characterized as cold or hot, dry or moist. The constellations stood to one another in various relations—in conjunction, opposition, sextile, quadrature, and trine. Some of these 'aspects' were held to be lucky (e. g., sextile and trine); the rest unlucky. The planets, in their courses along the zodiac, could stand similarly in good or bad relations to one another. To each planet a constellation was assigned as its 'house' (*domicilium*), another as its 'exaltation' (*altitudo*), still another as its 'fall' or 'dejection' (*dejectio*). Each sign of 30°, furthermore, contained a number of smaller divisions (faces, terms, decans), which were allotted to the planets as so many miniature 'exaltations' and 'dejections.' The horizon and the meridian were also of importance; their points of intersection were called the four pivots: 1. the ascendant, i. e., the point of the ecliptic on the eastern horizon at a given moment (the Greek name for this point, ὡροσκόπος, has come to be applied to the whole process of determining the fate of an individual at birth); 2. the intersection of the ecliptic with the lower meridian (*imum cœlum*); 3. the culminating point (*medium cœlum*), or intersection of the ecliptic with the upper meridian; 4. the descending point (*occidens, occasus*), or the point of the ecliptic vanishing on the western horizon. The arcs of the ecliptic contained between these pivots were each divided into three equal parts by means of circles of declination; the ecliptic was

it was not so successful with respect to its practical details. The inherent absurdity of many of its doctrines was, in fact, only too evident. 'What,' says Sextus Empiricus, 'have the arbitrary names given to the constellations of the zodiac to do with the actions and habits of man? What possible connection can exist between the celestial Lion and a warrior's bravery, or between the Virgin and a white skin? Can anything be more absurd than to make of the Bull a feminine sign?' Astrology had to admit that the names of the constellations were arbitrary. The name, astrology contended, served as a metaphor to indicate the nature of a constellation's influence—and this, in turn, had been discovered in the course of long experience.[1] Such an answer, however, stumbled against another embarrassing question: What about the vaunted age of the science? Astrologers claimed for it centuries of careful experiment,

thus composed of twelve sections, called the twelve celestial houses, which formed the basis of every astrological calculation. The astrologer, in reading a horoscope, first determined the position of the planets and constellations at the exact moment of birth, with reference to these twelve celestial houses—a task of no slight difficulty, since a planet shifts from one house to the succeeding one in the space of two hours. Each house ruled over a particular phase of man's life; one represented wealth, another sickness, another marriage, and so on. If, for instance, an evil planet (Saturn or Mars) stood in the house which represented wealth, the astrologer would have to predict poverty for his client, or at least advise thrift. If a beneficent star, such as Venus, happened to stand in the house of marriage, he might prophesy that riches would come by way of a dowry. The complex relations which planets and constellations were supposed to hold toward one another at a given moment, and the infinite variety of interpretations to which any horoscope could be subjected, served admirably for maintaining that judicious vagueness characteristic of all astrological prediction, which prevented it from being submitted to a final pragmatic test.

[1] Bouché-Leclercq, pp. 579-80. To ridicule the names given to the constellations became the fashion with the Church Fathers. See below, p. 20.

and named as its founders the gods themselves. 'Some pretend,' says Cicero, 'that the Chaldean astrologers have verified the nativities of children by calculations and experiments over a period of 470,000 years.' This, he maintains, is clearly impossible. 'Had they been in the habit of doing so, they would never have given up the practice. But, as a matter of fact, no author remains who knows of such a thing being done now, or ever having been done.'[1] Still, assertion could be met by assertion, and there was no dearth of astrologers who were willing to cite texts of any desired mythological age. Before the tribunal of an uncritical public their word was seldom questioned.

Nowhere could the critics find a more alluring opportunity to attack the doctrines of astrology than in connection with judicial[2] astrology itself. An art founded upon wrong axioms must of necessity fail in the execution; hence astrology, when practised commercially, has always tempted the satirist. The opponents of astrology confronted the reader of horoscopes with the bold assertion that his art was impossible. How, it was asked, could the astrologer ascertain with sufficient exactness the moment of birth, or the precise point of the heavenly sphere appearing above the horizon? To determine both of these to the minutest fraction was surely necessary: how else explain the unlike fates of twins? If the heavens moved so swiftly that twins could be born under totally different horoscopes, was it not clearly impossible to cast any nativity whatsoever? And if the moment of conception, as the astrologers asserted, had an importance only second to that of birth, the question of twins became in itself puzzling.[3] Again,

---

[1] Cicero, *De Divinatione* 2. 45.

[2] The term usually applied to the practical art of predicting the future from the configuration of the stars at birth.

[3] Schmekel, pp. 156, 159 ff.; Bouché-Leclercq, pp. 588 ff. The argument concerning twins was exceedingly popular. It is found

why limit predictions by the stars to the human race? 'If,' says Cicero, 'the aspect of the stars influences the birth of every human being, it should, by parity of reasoning, determine the fates of beasts as well; yet what can be more absurd?' Sextus Empiricus pictures the discomfiture of an astrologer faced by a man and an ass, both born under the same sign; and Favorinus smiles at the consistent astrologer casting the horoscopes of mice and flies.[1]

None of these objections, however, greatly embarrassed the defenders of astrology. The difficulties of observation, no one more willingly conceded than the astrologer himself. He was thereby assured an escape when his predictions failed, and a double glory when he was successful. Ptolemy frankly admitted that the practice of judicial astrology was difficult, but contended, too, that the mistakes of charlatans should not be laid at the door of the science. The question of twins, furthermore, troubled only the theorists. For the popular mind it was enough that a double birth deserved a double horoscope. The attempt, finally, to ridicule astrology by demanding that it extend its functions to include the animal kingdom, was only a proof of the critic's ignorance. Astrology in time extended its sway, not only over the animal kingdom, but over the vegetable and mineral as well.[2]

One criticism directed against judicial astrology by Carneades and his followers remains to be considered. It occupied an important place in the argument, and was afterwards employed effectively by the Church. It asked of astrology this question: If the destinies of all men are determined by the stars, how explain the similar fates of large groups of individuals born in the most various cir-

---

in Cicero (*Divin.* 2. 43), in Favorinus (Aulus Gellius 14. 1. 26). and in Sextus Empiricus. We shall find it again in Augustine (*Civ. Dei* 5. 6), who popularized it for the Middle Ages.

[1] Bouché-Leclercq, pp. 585-6; Cicero, *Divin.* 2. 46.

[2] Bouché-Leclercq, pp. 586, 591.

cumstances? 'Were all those who perished at the battle of Cannæ,' demands Cicero, 'born under the same star?' 'Were all the barbarians killed at Marathon,' asks Sextus Empiricus, 'born under the arrow of Sagittarius, and all the heroes drowned at Salamis, under the sign of the Water-carrier?' Again, if the constellation Virgo bestows upon those born under its domain a white skin, must one conclude that no Ethiopian is born in the month of August? These questions were perplexing—astrology did not answer some of them successfully until it had embodied in its doctrine a system of astrological ethnology, such as is found in the second book of Ptolemy's *Tetrabiblos*. We have already seen that, in his introductory defense of astrology, Ptolemy claimed for general catastrophes an unequivocal precedence over all individual destinies. And in the second book, a solution is offered of the geographic problem as well. Ptolemy placed the various divisions of the globe under the dominion of separate planets and constellations, and these geographic influences he pronounced of greater potency than the horoscopes of the individual. In favor of his system, Ptolemy cited precisely the black skin of the Ethiopian, and the white skin of the Teuton and the Gaul.[1]

Like Hydra or Proteus, astrology remained after each assault stronger than ever. In truth, its foundations had been hardly shaken. Belief in astrology could be destroyed only by an attack on its source—either by proving that an influence of the stars on human life did not exist, or by demonstrating that such an influence was unknowable. The opponents of astrology, by expending their energies in assaults on the outposts, and failing to attack the citadel, only strengthened the belief that the latter was unconquerable.

[1] Bouché-Leclercq, pp. 581 ff.; Schmekel, p. 157; Cicero, *Divin.* 2. 44; *Claudii Ptolemæi Opera,* pp. 392 ff. On Ptolemy, see also Boll, pp. 181 ff.

During the first centuries of our era, while Christianity's attack upon it was still in preparation, astrology spread everywhere through the Roman world.[1] Emperors from Augustus to Alexander Severus consulted the Chaldeans, and among the common people its vogue was universal. None of the ancient arts of divination remained free from its taint. Poets from Juvenal to Ammianus Marcellinus satirized the extravagant worship paid to it by the fashionable public. Astrological ideas were in the air. Cicero, who as philosopher fulminated against astrology, as rhetorician subscribed to its principles. When, in the *Somnium Scipionis,* he calls Jupiter 'a star that brings health and prosperity to the race of men,' and Mars 'a planet red, and feared on earth,' he accepts the very axioms of the science.[2] Seneca, being a Stoic, is naturally a firm believer in astrology; Tacitus, though he satirizes the astrologers of the court, is only half convinced that astrology itself is a deception.[3] And when, in the second century, it won as a convert the greatest astronomer of the ancient world, little was left for it to conquer; with Ptolemy ancient astrology found its last and most famous spokesman. The late prose writer, Firmicus Maternus, though he has left in his *Mathesis* the longest ancient treatise on astrology, and contributes—especially in the first and eighth books— to our knowledge of the philosophical defense of the science, really offers nothing new.

With the almost universal theoretical acceptance of astrology was joined, however, a general distrust of the astrologer himself. The commercial practitioner stood low in the social scale, and was often a mere charlatan. Astrology in practice, furthermore, was seldom dissociated from necromancy and vulgar magic, and the astrologer in time

[1] Bouché-Leclercq, pp. 146-80.
[2] *Somn. Scip.*, chap. 4.
[3] *Annales* 6. 22.

became a public nuisance. As early as Augustus, laws were enacted against the *Chaldæi* and the *mathematici,* and succeeding rulers issued decrees of increasing severity. An emperor might himself wish to make use of the astrologer, but feared him when in the employ of new candidates for the throne. At times a distinction was made between the practice and the science—*professionem eorum, non notitiam, esse prohibitum,* reads one enactment[1]—but after the close of the third century the absolute interdiction of astrology, formulated by Diocletian, and embodied in the Theodosian code, remained permanently on the statute-books.[2] In the eyes of the public, of course, persecution of the astrologer only enhanced the value of his art, and in itself implied belief in its efficacy. The strange inconsistency of the ancient attitudes toward astrologers is best preserved, perhaps, in the famous sentence of Tacitus, in which he calls them 'dangerous to princes, and a fallacious reliance to ambitious subjects—a race of men which in our state will ever be both shunned and retained.'[3]

II

So it was that when Christianity, at the close of the second century, began to assume a position of prominence in the social and intellectual life of the Roman Empire, it found astrology everywhere, battening on the superstitions both of populace and kings. The Church attacked astrology with all available weapons. The reasons for its hostility are fairly obvious. As a part of paganism, the practice of all divinatory arts was forbidden the Christian; and, in the writings of the earlier apologists, astrology is hardly

[1] Bouché-Leclercq, p. 566.
[2] *Ibid.*
[3] Tacitus, *Hist.* 1. 22: 'Genus hominum potentibus infidum, sperantibus fallax, quod in civitate nostra et vetabitur semper et retinebitur.'

differentiated from soothsaying, oracles, and magic. In its philosophical dress, astrology was even less acceptable. The fatalism implied in the belief that the stars are arbiters of human destinies never found more unyielding opponents than the Church Fathers. The methods of attack varied somewhat through the centuries, and the conclusions arrived at by the Western Church differed considerably from those reached by the writers of the more scientific East. The Christian apologists, moreover, seldom satisfied the demands of strict logic itself; the reader is often surprised to find astrology readmitted into orthodox doctrine by some unguarded concession. But the war, though often waged with naïve and unscientific arguments, was always persistent; and its success was such that after Augustine, in his trenchant condemnation of astrological divination, had finally formulated the doctrine of the Western Church, astrology virtually disappeared from the social and intellectual life of western Europe for eight centuries.[1]

The Christians maintained, in general, that all divinatory arts, and, above all, astrology, were inventions of the devil, and could be carried on only by the aid of demons. This theory arose early, and remained throughout the Middle Ages the argument of last resort. A belief in the power and prevalence of demons was universal in primitive Christianity. Paul identifies the fallen angels (1 Cor. 20-1)[2] with the heathen gods; the Old Testament stories of Saul and the witch, and of the Egyptian magicians, were cited as proof that they were concerned in occult arts. It was an easy saving of argument, therefore, to admit at the outset the possibility of astrological prediction, and, at the same

[1] The final pages of Bouché-Leclercq's *L'Astrologie Grecque* (pp. 609-27) contain a concise discussion of the combat of the early Church with astrology. On the attitude of Christianity toward ancient divination as a whole, cf. Bouché-Leclercq, *Histoire de la Divination* 1. 92-104.

[2] Cf. Lev. 17. 7; Deut. 32. 17; 2 Chron. 11. 15.

time, to prohibit its use by asserting that it could only be accomplished through diabolic aid.[1]

But danger lurked in pushing this theory too far; for how could even demons read the future in the stars unless it was written there? And how distinguish between a prediction through the help of evil spirits and one sanctioned by God?[2] The first chapter of Genesis (1. 14) could be cited to prove that the heavenly bodies were placed in the sky for the express purpose of serving as signs; and there were examples in Biblical history where God himself had made use of astrological predictions: witness the miracle of Hezekiah's pillar, the star of the Magi, the darkening of the sun at Christ's death, and the celestial signs which were to announce his return. The star of the Magi, in particular, was a stumbling-block, and many were the attempts to explain it. The early Fathers, Ignatius and

---

[1] The texts are many. Lactantius (*Divinarum Institutionum* 2. 17) affords a convenient quotation: 'Eorum [dæmones] inventa sunt astrologia, et aruspicina, et auguratio, et necromantia, et ars magica, et quiquid præterea malorum exercent homines, vel palam vel occulte' (Migne, *Patr. Lat.* 6. 336). According to Tatian (*Oratio ad Græcos,* chap. 9), demons, impersonating the heathen gods, made people believe that they had been carried to the sky, and were embodied in the planets and constellations. Origen (*Comment. in Matth.* 13. 6) explains the apparent success of cures effected by medical astrologers as due to demons, who watch the phases of the moon to enter their victims. We shall meet the theory fully developed in Augustine; see below, p. 23. Cf. Bouché-Leclercq, p. 610.

[2] A belief, arising among certain Christian sects, that there were good demons as well as bad, rendered the Church doctrine extremely dangerous. The Priscillianists—a sect of the fourth century—made patriarchs of the signs of the zodiac, and angels of the planets. A special canon at the council of Braga, in 561, was directed against them. In the Middle Ages, the magic of the Jewish Cabala and the learned necromancy of the Moors rested upon a similar belief that the world of spirits could be rendered innocuous. Cf. Bouché-Leclercq, pp. 623-4; La Ville de Mirmont, *L'Astrologie chez les Gallo-Romains,* p. 113 (*Bibliothèque des Universités du Midi,* Vol. 7).

Tertullian, did not deny that it went far toward sanction-
ing astrology. According to their theory, all divinatory
arts had been permitted by God until the coming of Christ,
when an end was put to the rule of demons over the world.
In the persons of the Magi, therefore, astrology had come
to abdicate at the cradle of the Redeemer; the return of
the Magi to their home by a different route indicated that
henceforth its employment was forbidden.[1]

But the orthodoxy of Tertullian's naïve admission became
suspect in the later centuries, and more uncompromising
arguments were deemed necessary. In the Church of
the East—especially in the writings of Basil and Chrysostom—a new exegesis was put forth, in which it was asserted
that the star of the Magi was no ordinary star at all, nor
even a planet or comet. Chrysostom cleverly turns against
the astrologers their own doctrines. It is the task of
astrology to predict the destinies of the child after it is
born, not to prophesy the birth itself. The appearance of
the star, he says, was a miracle, and outside the normal
course of events. Proof that it was no common star consisted in the fact that it moved, not from east to west, but
from north to south—the way Palestine lies with regard
to Persia.[2]

[1] Ignatius, *Epist. ad Ephes.* 19; Tertullian, *De Idolatria*, chap. 9:
'Sed magi et astrologi ab Oriente venerunt. Scimus magiæ et
astrologiæ inter se societatem. Primi igitur stellarum interpretes
natum Christum annuntiaverunt, primi muneraverunt. Quid tum?
Ideo nunc et mathematicis patrocinabitur illorum magorum religio?
De Christo scilicet est mathesis hodie; stellas Christi, non Saturni
et Martis et cujusque ex eodem ordine mortuorum observat et
prædicat. At enim scientia ista usque ad Evangelium fuit concessa,
ut, Christo edito, nemo exinde nativitatem alicujus de cælo interpretaretur' (Migne, *Patr. Lat.* 1. 672). The last sentence of this
quotation constitutes a portion of Isidore's definition of astrology
(*Etymol.* 8. 9. 23). It was repeated many times through the Middle
Ages. Cf. below, pp. 27-8, 30-2.

[2] Basil, *Hom.* 25; Chrysostom, *Hom. in Matth.* 6. For other
citations, see Bouché-Leclercq, p. 613, note 1.

The Eastern Church, in general, formulated a more scientific doctrine concerning astrology than that current in the West. Origen, together with the Gnostics, even effected a compromise between astrology and Christianity, so that, when purged of fatalistic doctrines, it was allowed to exist without interference. Origen's one concern was to disprove a deterministic influence of the stars; even divine fore-knowledge, he maintained, did not abrogate free will. That the stars cannot be the cause of human destinies, Origen proved by an ingenious argument. It is the characteristic of every cause that it precedes its effect. Now, inasmuch as the configuration of the stars does not precede, but is at best concomitant with, the birth over which it presides, how can the stars be the cause of the child's fortunes? Origen accepts with no remonstrance, however, the Neo-platonic doctrine that the stars, though not causing human events, constitute the signs by which they can be foretold. This theory, developed fully by Plotinus, goes back through Philo to an astrological interpretation of the fourteenth verse of the opening chapter of Genesis. Origen, to be sure, like the Neoplatonists, was wise enough not to attempt its proof.[1]

Origen and the Gnostics did not yield to a compromise with astrology before they had exhausted the ancient store of arguments against it. We meet again the dispute concerning twins, the argument that astrological observation is impossible, and the contention that the judicial astrologer takes no account of geographic and racial considerations. The last argument even received a clever enlargement—perhaps the one contribution of Christian writers to the

---

[1] The fullest statement of Origen's attitude toward astrology is found in Eusebius' *Præparatio Evangelica* 6. 11 (Migne, *Patr. Gr.* 21. 478 ff.). Plotinus' compromise with astrology (Bouché-Leclercq, p. 600; Zeller, *Phil. der Griechen* 3. 567) tempted many Church writers. See below, pp. 22, 38, 57.

discussion. Astrology had explained similarities of race by means of a system of astrological geography, placing each country under the sway of separate planets and stars. But, said the Christian writers, are racial characteristics really dependent upon geography? The Jews circumcise on the eighth day in Rome as in Palestine; have they carried the Judæan stars with them, or have they been freed from their influence? And the Christians, are they not scattered over all the globe, and yet suffer the same fortunes? It is not worth while to ask how astrology might have replied to these new questions. Inasmuch as Origen and the Gnostics ended by virtually accepting astrology, a refutation was, perhaps, deemed unnecessary.[1]

In the Western Church, the one great opponent of astrology was Augustine. Coming in contact with astrologers early in life, as he tells us in his *Confessions,* he was at first attracted to them, preferring them to the soothsayers, because they invoked no spirits. Even the warning of a physician, who told him that astrology was a fraud, passed unheeded. Only after a friend had set him to pondering over the astrological problem concerning twins did Augustine, too, decide that astrological divination was a mere matter of chance.[2] Henceforth astrology had in him a sworn enemy. Again and again he attacked it in his writings, repeating the dialectic of Carneades,[3] and adding the

[1] The discussion of astrology by the Gnostic Bardesanes (Eusebius, *Præp. Ev.* 6. 10: Migne, *Patr. Gr.* 21. 467 ff.) parallels that of Origen almost throughout. It is Bardesanes who asks the question concerning the Jews (Migne, *Patr. Gr.* 21. 475). A third series of similar arguments is found in the *Recognitiones* of Clement (9. 12—10. 13). Cf. Bouché-Leclercq, pp. 534-5, 615-6.

[2] *Confessions* 4. 3, and 7. 6.

[3] Augustine points to the absurdity of putting faith in the arbitrary names given to the constellations (*De Doctr. Christ.* 2. 21)—an argument found in other Christian writers; cf. Tatian, *Oratio ad Græcos,* chap. 9; Hippolytus, *Refutatio Omnium Hæresium* 4. 24; Basil, *Hom. in Hex.* 6. 6. Augustine also questions the right of

vehemence of his own rhetoric. Especially did he never tire of illustrating the problem of twins; one is compelled to smile at the seriousness with which he employed this mediocre argument. He confronts the astrologer with the historic case of Jacob and Esau, and asks him how the heavens can be held to account for the enormous difference in the destinies alloted to two children born so nearly at the same time. He ridicules the theory that the movement of the spheres is swift enough to make of the one a desert-wanderer, and of the other the father of a mighty people. Twins, again, are sick at the same time. The fact is explained by the physician, Hippocrates, as due to a similarity of temperaments, and by the Stoic, Posidonius, as due to an identity of horoscopes. Augustine sees here an opportunity to confute the astrologer with his own doctrine. 'Why,' he asks, 'were they both sick of the same disease, and at the same time, and not the one after the other in the order of their birth, inasmuch as they could not have been born simultaneously? Or, if the fact of their having been born at different times does not necessarily imply that they must be sick at different times, why do the astrologers contend that the difference in the time of their births was the cause of their difference in other things?'[1] It is not necessary to examine the score of ways in which astrology might have answered Augustine's questions. In general, it probably refused to quarrel over such minutiæ, and might have considered it a sufficient answer to ask Augustine, in turn, whence, if not from the stars themselves, could come

astrologers to deny horoscopes to animals (*Civ. Dei* 5. 7). He has something to say on the star of the Magi in *Ad Faustum* (2. 5).

[1] *Civ. Dei* 5. 4-5 (Migne, *Patr. Lat.* 41. 144); cf. *De Genesi ad Litteram* 2. 17 (Migne, *Patr. Lat.* 34. 278). A. Schmekel (*Die Philosophie der Mittleren Stoa*, pp. 162 ff.) has proved that the refutation of astrology found in the first chapters of Augustine's *De Civitate Dei* is based on a lost portion of Cicero's *De Fato*, which, in turn, like the *De Divinatione*, goes back to Carneades; see above, p. 6.

that general similarity of temperament which, in the alternative theory of the physician, he himself accepted.

What end, one may ask, did Augustine have in view in his struggle against astrology? Was it the same as that of the pagan Sceptics and Origen—to defend the freedom of the human will? It may appear so at first. Augustine, too, maintains that the actions of man are free from the arbitrary rule of the stars, and praises the pagan philosophers for defending the ethical responsibility of man.[1] But it soon becomes clear that his purpose is only that of replacing astrological fatalism by an even more stringent deterministic doctrine—the theory of predestination and divine foreknowledge. Those who, like Cicero, deny prediction of the future altogether, receive at the hands of Augustine a more violent condemnation than the astrologers themselves.[2] So occupied, in truth, is Augustine with combating fatalism, that he is almost ready to accept astrology when, in the Neoplatonic form, it rids itself of this noxious doctrine. He objects to the theory of Plotinus, however, on the score that no astrologer actually accepts the stars as mere indicators of events, and that it, too, does not obviate the practical difficulties involved in the matter of twins.[3]

In spite of his denunciation of astrology as a fatalistic science, and his contention that it is impossible in practice, Augustine never seriously defends the scepticism once expressed in the *Confessions*. After exhausting his dialectic powers in destroying astrology as a legitimate art,

[1] *Ad Faustum* 2. 5; *De Genesi ad Litteram* 2. 17; *Civ. Dei* 5. 1.

[2] Augustine (*Civ. Dei* 5. 9) mentions Cicero by name. He detested him even more than the Stoics, simply because, in denying the possibility of divination, he denied the existence of God: 'Multo sunt autem tolerabiliores qui vel sidera fata constituunt, quam iste, qui tollit præscientiam futurorum. Nam et confiteri esse Deum, et negare præscium futurorum, apertissima insania est' (Migne, *Patr. Lat.* 41. 149).

[3] *Civ. Dei* 5. 1 (Migne, *Patr. Lat.* 41. 142).

he ends by accepting the possibility of astrological predictions if made by the help of demons. 'All these things considered'—so Augustine closes the discussion—'we have good reason to believe that, when the astrologers give very many wonderful answers, it is to be attributed to the occult inspiration of spirits, not of the best kind, whose care it is to creep into the minds of men, and to confirm in them false and noxious opinions concerning the fatal influence of the stars, and that it is not due to their marking and inspecting of horoscopes, according to a kind of art which in reality has no existence.'[1] With Augustine, in fact, the discussion of astrology in the early Church returned to its point of departure. For Augustine, as for Tertullian and Lactantius, astrology was merely one of many nefarious practices with which the hosts of fallen angels tried to cheat mankind. In a special treatise—the *De Divinatione Dæmonum*—Augustine crystallized the doctrine of the early Church regarding the powers of demons, and laid the foundation for those mediæval superstitions which bore malignant fruit in the magic and witchcraft of the fifteenth century. Astrology, refused the name of a science, was forced to live under its ignominious stigma until, in the thirteenth century, it forced a revision of the Church's verdict.[2]

An observant eye, however, might have discovered even in the *De Civitate Dei* the germs of that new compromise between Christianity and astrology which was to find expression in the *Summa Theologiæ* of Thomas Aquinas and the *Divina Commedia* of Dante. In his preoccupation

[1] *Civ. Dei* 5. 7 (Migne, *Patr. Lat.* 41. 147).

[2] Bouché-Leclercq, *L'Astrologie Grecque*, p. 623; Bouché-Leclercq, *Histoire de la Divination* 1. 99 ff. The *De Divinatione Dæmonum* (Migne, *Patr. Lat.* 40. 581) explains how the demons obtain knowledge of the future by reason of their superior spiritual powers, and by permission of God himself. On the importance for later witchcraft of the Church-doctrine concerning demons, see J. Hansen, *Zauberwahn, Inquisition, und Hexenprozess im Mittelalter* (Munich and Leipzig, 1900).

with the practical details of astrology as a divinatory art, Augustine failed to note his own unconscious concessions to it as a physical science—concessions which could be made the basis for an almost complete rehabilitation. Into the midst of his discussion of the astrological dilemma concerning twins, he inserts this passage: 'It is not altogether absurd to say that certain sidereal influences have some power to cause differences in bodies alone. We see, for instance, that the seasons of the year vary as the sun approaches and recedes, and that certain things are increased or diminished in size by the waxings and wanings of the moon, such as sea-urchins, oysters, and the wonderful ocean-tides. But it does not follow that the wills of men are subject to the configuration of the stars.'[1] Though in the form of a negative statement, this passage contains in embryo the solution of the astrological problem as it was formulated by the theologians of the thirteenth century.

[1] *Civ. Dei* 5. 6 (Migne, *Patr. Lat.* 41. 146). An admission that the stars influence the atmosphere, and consequently may produce modifications in the physical constitution and habits of man, is made also by Sextus Empiricus (Bouché-Leclercq, p. 595, note 1). On the basis of such a concession, a clever psychologist could restore almost the entire science.

CHAPTER II

ASTROLOGY IN THE EARLY MEDIÆVAL CENTURIES

In the general decline of learning which overtook Western Europe during the first mediæval centuries, no science suffered a more complete eclipse than astrology. Even in its popular manifestations, astrology was a learned superstition, and demanded a high state of civilization for its development—a condition which manifestly could not exist at a time when barbarians ruled the Roman Empire. Christianity, moreover, through the efforts of the Church Fathers, had set itself directly against all divinatory arts, and the newly Christianized peoples of the North could not be expected to object to the Church's verdict. Astrology's legitimate sister, astronomy, fared much better during the Dark Ages. The needs of daily life, and the exigencies arising out of the Paschal controversy, gave to astronomical studies a fair impetus, which bore fruit in such scientific writings as those of Bede. The revival of astrology, on the other hand, like that of pagan philosophy and literature itself, was a much more gradual one. Not until the twelfth century, with its discovery of Aristotle and the science of the Moors, did astrology regain a position of prominence in the intellectual life of Europe.

The slight knowledge of astrology which the Middle Ages preserved out of the wreckage of the ancient world was drawn, in the first instance, from the writings of the Church Fathers themselves. Astrology had played so prominent a part in the struggle of early Christianity against paganism that it could not but find its way into those popularizations of patristic learning which constituted the chief literary product of the first mediæval centuries. Here and there, throughout the Middle Ages, discussions on astrology continued to appear in connection with an exegesis of the

star of the Magi or a sermon on fatalism, even though the
writers might entertain for astrology itself merely an academic interest.   It is thus in a homily on the Epiphany that
Gregory finds occasion to discuss astrology.   He directs
his attack particularly against the Priscillianists,[1] a Gnostic
sect of Spain accused of magic.   He repeats the classic
argument of twins, using Augustine's illustration of Jacob
and Esau, and points again to the impossibility of squaring
judicial astrology with ethnological influences.[2]   Yet one
feels at once that with Gregory astrology is no longer a
living issue.   Even Priscillianism dated back to the time of
Augustine and Ambrose.   Astrology had fallen on evil days,
and it was mentioned only by way of literary reminiscence.
Cassiodorus speaks of it briefly in two passages, calling it
a 'slippery error,' and citing Augustine and Basil as proof
that its doctrines lead to heresy.[3]   Boethius, in whose *Con-
solation of Philosophy* one might expect to find a full discussion of astrological fatalism, honors it with one slight
allusion.[4]   And Macrobius exhibits veritable embarrassment
when he is called upon to explain the passage of the
Somnium Scipionis where Cicero describes the astrological
characteristics of the planets.[5]   He is able to discuss the

[1] See above, p. 17.

[2] Gregory, *Homilia XX: In Die Epiphania* (Migne, *Patr. Lat.*
76. 1111).   In illustrating his second argument, Gregory asks the
astrologers why, if Aquarius produces fishermen, no children are
born under that sign in Getulia, an inland country, and why
there are many peoples without bankers, if Libra is the constellation
of the money-changers.

[3] Cassiodorus, *Expositio in Psalterium CXLVIII* (Migne, *Patr.
Lat.* 70. 1047); *De Artibus ac Disciplinis Liberalium Litterarium,*
chap. 7 (Migne, *Patr. Lat.* 70. 1218).

[4] Boethius, *Cons. Phil.* 4. 6.

[5] Macrobius, *Somn. Scip.* 1. 19. 20 (ed. Janus, Leipzig, 1848,
p. 70).   Macrobius became in the eleventh century an important
authority on astronomical questions (see below, p. 32).   He and
Chalcidius, whose commentary on the *Timæus* was based on one
by Posidonius, even preserved the Aristotelian doctrine that the

philosophical aspect of astrology at some length, and even gives an outline of the Platonic myth of the creation of man by the planetary gods; but when he tries to expound the astrological facts themselves, he is clearly puzzled. He confesses that the only treatise he has ever read on the subject is Ptolemy's *Harmonia,* and he proceeds, accordingly, to explain the evil influence of Saturn and the benevolent character of Jupiter by means of a complicated system of numbers.

No writer did so much to fasten upon the Middle Ages the patristic condemnation of astrology as the encyclopædist of the seventh century, Isidore of Seville; and the several passages of the *Etymologiæ* and the *De Natura Rerum* that bear on astrology deserve careful scrutiny. Important, first of all, is his definition of astrology itself. Astrology, he says, is partly *naturalis,* and partly *superstitiosa.* Natural astrology is only another name for astronomy. Superstitious astrology, on the other hand, 'is that science which is practised by the *mathematici,* who read prophecies in the heavens, and who place the twelve constellations as rulers over the members of man's body and soul, and who predict the nativities and dispositions of men by the courses of the stars.'[1] The *mathematici* and *genethliaci* reappear in a later chapter of the *Etymologiæ* in company with many other representatives of magic. Here again Isidore refers to their art as superstitious, and identifies them with the Magi of the Gospel—'cuius artis scientia usque ad Evangelium fuit concessa, ut, Christo edito, nemo exinde nativitatem alicuius de cælo interpretaretur.' The last sentence of this definition Isidore quoted

---

double movement of the heavens causes generation and corruption on earth (*Commentarius in Timæum,* chap. 75: ed. Mullach, *Fragmenta Philosophorum,* Paris, 1881, 2. 198); cf. Switalski, *Des Chalcidius Commentar zu Platos Timæus,* Münster, 1902, pp. 28 ff. (in Bäumker's *Beiträge* 3. 6).

[1] *Etymol.* 3. 27 (Migne, *Patr. Lat.* 82. 170).

from Tertullian, though with little understanding of its context. It remained throughout the Middle Ages an integral part of the stock definition of astrologers.[1] But Isidore's logic is hardly equal to his learning. Several curious bits of astrological lore smuggled themselves into his writings, and became the common property of the succeeding centuries. Astrological medicine, for example, which Isidore condemns in his definition of superstitious astrology, he accepts, in part at least, in a later chapter.[2] The good physician, he says, will study astronomy as well as his own art, inasmuch as it is well known that our bodies change with the varying state of the weather and the stars. In the *De Natura Rerum,* Isidore ascribes to the moon an influence over fruits, over the brains of animals, and over oysters and sea-urchins. He even refers to it, in a phrase of unmistakable astrological coloring, as the *dux humentium substantiarum.*[3] The dog-star is said to be a cause of sickness.[4] As for comets, Isidore accepts them without reserve as the prognosticators of revolution, war, and pestilence.[5]

Isidore and the elder Pliny are the principal sources for the scientific works of Bede, and are severally responsible for two of the slight astrological references discoverable in his writings. It is upon Pliny that Bede draws for a chapter on the planets in the *De Natura Rerum.* Probably with no

---

[1] *Etymol.* 8. 9. 23 (Migne, *Patr. Lat.* 82. 313). Cf. above, p. 18.

[2] *Etymol.* 4. 13. 4 (Migne 82. 198).

[3] *De Nat. Rer.* 18. 6; 19. 2 (Migne, *Patr. Lat.* 83. 992). Isidore borrowed the passage from Ambrose's *Hexaemeron* (4. 7. 29-30: Migne, *Patr. Lat.* 14. 215).

[4] *De Nat. Rer.* 16. 14 (Migne, *Patr. Lat.* 83. 1000).

[5] 'Hæc cum nascitur, aut regni mutationem fertur ostendere, aut bella, aut pestilentias surgere' (*De Nat. Rer.* 26. 13: Migne, *Patr. Lat.* 83. 1000). The astrological significance of comets seems to have been accepted generally in the early Church; cf. Bouché-Leclercq, p. 623; J. H. Robinson, *The Great Comet of 1680: A Study in the History of Rationalism* (Northfield, Minn., 1916), pp. 5-6.

consciousness that he is trespassing upon the domain of astrology, he follows his author in characterizing Saturn as cold, Jupiter as temperate, and Mars as glowing. It is curious to note, however, that he stops here, and omits Pliny's astrological description of Venus as the planet which nourishes all things on earth.[1] Isidore, in turn, is responsible for Bede's chapter on comets. There is, in fact, evidence in several of his works that he was a firm believer in their prophetic virtue. In the *Ecclesiastical History*, for instance, the comets of 729 are connected with the inroad of the Saracens into Gaul, and with the deaths of king Osric and the holy Egbert.[2]

One condemnation of astrology proper is found in Bede's works. Its source I have not discovered. It occurs in a passage of the *De Temporum Ratione*, which comments on the division of time into hours, minutes, and seconds. The *mathematici*, says Bede, continue the division to still smaller units. Since, however, their science is vain, and contrary to the Christian faith, he will refrain from using their terminology.[3]

Isidore is again a source for the encyclopædist of the ninth century, Rabanus Maurus, Bishop of Fulda. The latter's chief scientific work, the *De Universo*, contains a chapter on magic which is a literal transcript of that in Isidore's *Etymologiæ*. *Astrologi* and *mathematici* are classed, as in the latter, among necromancers and augurs; and Rabanus subscribes to the Tertullianist doctrine that

[1] Bede, *De Nat. Rer.*, chap. 13 (Migne, *Patr. Lat.* 90. 211); cf. Pliny, *Nat. Hist.* 2. 6.

[2] Bede repeats Isidore's description of comets word for word (*De Nat. Rer.*, chap. 24: Migne, *Patr. Lat.* 90. 243). Comets are spoken of in the *Historia Ecclesiastica* 4. 12, and 5. 23, 24 (ed. Plummer, Oxford, 1896, 1. 118, 349, 356).

[3] Bede, *De Temp. Rat.*, chap. 3 (Migne, *Patr. Lat.* 90. 305). Cf. the mild rebuke of astrology which is found in a letter of Aldhelm (Bishop of Sherborne, 640-709), quoted by William of Malmesbury (*Anglia Sacra* 2. 7.).

astrology, though permitted till the birth of Christ, was thenceforth a forbidden science.[1] Isidore's chapter on magic was copied in another work of Rabanus, the *De Magicis Artibus,* the longest treatise on divination which had appeared since Augustine.[2] Rabanus presents the general views of the Church Fathers on the subject of demons, and the rôle they were supposed to play in divination. This treatise, in fact, was destined to exert an important influence on the growing body of Church law on the subject of sorcery and magic.[3] Christianity, from the time of its introduction among the barbarian peoples of the North, had proceeded to combat pagan magic and witchcraft. The early Penitentials are replete with references to occult practices. It was probably in answer to a demand for a systematized doctrine on the subject that such treatises as that of Rabanus were written. And when the great canonists of the succeeding centuries came to deal with the subjects of sorcery and magic, they followed the lead of Rabanus Maurus, also basing their utterances on the doctrine of demonology formulated by the early Church. The *Decretum* of Burchard, Bishop of Worms in the first quarter of the eleventh century, quotes freely from the works of Augustine and Isidore—particularly from the former's *De Divinatione Dæmonum.* Astrology is found again in the list of magic practices borrowed from Isidore,[4] Burchard's *Decretum,* as is well known, was embodied with little change in the collections of Church law of Ivo of Chartres and Gratian. On the subject of astrology, all three are in virtual agreement. Gratian, it is true, adds an excerpt from Augustine's *De Doctrina Christiana,* and quotes a Church law against observing the stars for the purpose of planting seed or contracting a marriage. But

[1] *De Universo* 15. 4 (Migne, *Patr. Lat.* III. 423).
[2] *De Magicis Artibus* (Migne, *Patr. Lat.* 110. 1098).
[3] Hansen, *Zauberwahn im Mittelalter,* p. 38.
[4] Burchard, *Decretum* 10. 43 (Migne, *Patr. Lat.* 140. 841).

Isidore's chapter on magic, with its definitions of the *mathematici* and *genethliaci,* still constitutes the longest reference to astrology.[1]

It is very doubtful whether any mediæval writer thus far cited had anything more than a literary acquaintance with astrology. The haruspices, augurs, and astrologers, so faithfully defined in every treatise on sorcery and magic from Isidore to Gratian, were probably as foreign to the actual life of the tenth and eleventh centuries as the religion of pagan Rome itself. But citations from the Fathers that might apply to the simple sorcery of the northern peoples were hard to find, and the canonists contented themselves with what lay ready to hand. The fact that the canon law classed astrology among the diabolic arts, or even discussed the subject at all, was probably, in the first instance, an accident. It became a matter of consequence only when the Church, in the course of the twelfth century, was again called upon to deal with astrologers in the flesh.

Even before the sudden arrival of Arabian science in the schools of Italy and France had brought the Church once more face to face with astrology, the latter had begun to find channels of literary transmission less narrow than those leading down through Isidore. The eleventh and twelfth centuries witnessed in France a general renaissance of Latin literature, and many a gleaning of scientific fact was made in the course of a promiscuous reading that did not have to wait for the rediscovery of Aristotle.[2] This newly awakened humanism found its best representatives

---

[1] Ivo of Chartres, *Decretum* 10. 68 (Migne, *Patr. Lat.* 161. 762) ; Gratian, *Decretum* 2. 26. 3-5 (Migne, *Patr. Lat.* 187. 1342 ff.). The list of the mediæval writers who repeated Isidore's definition of astrology is, of course, not exhausted. It is found in the *De Divinis Officiis,* ascribed to Alcuin (Migne, *Patr. Lat.* 101. 1178), and again in a twelfth-century treatise on cosmology, ascribed to Bede (Migne, *Patr. Lat.* 90. 908).

[2] Taylor, *The Mediæval Mind* (London, 1914) 2. 144.

in the famous school of Chartres.[1] From the time of Fulbert to that of John of Salisbury, the Chartres school was a leader in liberal and scientific studies, and even astrology was not omitted from the range of its interests. The curiosity of the mediæval classicist must have been aroused by many an astrological allusion in Lucan, Persius, or the writings of the Fathers. John of Salisbury, in repeating Isidore's traditional definition of astrology,[3] takes evident pleasure in illustrating it with choice bits quoted from the Latin satirists. In addition to such indirect information on astrological matters as they found in the Latin classics, the writers of the twelfth century had in their hands two direct sources for ancient astrology, the *Mathesis* of Firmicus, and the repositories of astrological Platonism, Chalcidius and Macrobius. Add to this the fact that the Chartres school, in the early half of the century, was already in possession of the first scientific treatises to reach northern Europe from Mohammedan Spain, and it is not surprising that astrological discussions became frequent.

As early as the year 1000—if the chronicles are to be believed[1]—Pope Sylvester II had studied Firmicus in Spain. A hundred years later there are indubitable traces of his presence in England. And, at the opening of the twelfth century, Firmicus Maternus is cited by name in a poem by Marbodus, who, as Bishop of Rennes, was connected indirectly with the school of Chartres. In the poetic discussion of astrology which constitutes a portion of his *Liber Decem Capitulorum,* Marbodus attacks Firmicus Maternus vigorously, repeating some of the stock arguments of the Fathers, and asserting particularly that his fatalistic doctrines destroy all ethics and all social order.[1] The influence of Firmicus

[1] Clerval, *Les Ecoles de Chartres au Moyen Age* (Chartres, 1895).

[2] *Policraticus* I. 12 (ed. Webb, Oxford, 1909, I. 52).

[3] Higden, *Polychronicon* (ed. Lumby, Rolls Ser.) 7. 68; William of Malmesbury, *De Gestis Regum Anglorum* 2. 167 (Migne, *Patr. Lat.* 179. 1138).

[4] Marbodus, *Liber Decem Capitulorum,* chap. 6: *De Fato et Genesi* (Migne, *Patr. Lat.* 171. 1704). Curiously enough, Marbodus

on the writers of the Chartres school itself can be clearly proved in the case of William of Conches (1080-1154), whose cosmological treatise, *De Philosophia Mundi,* couples his name with Ptolemy.[1]   His influence is apparent, too, in the *De Mundi Universitate* of Bernard Silvestris, a work of mingled prose and verse, composed between 1145 and 1153.   The eighth book of the *Mathesis* of Firmicus opens with a striking passage, in which man's superiority over the animal kingdom is illustrated by the fact that he walks erect, and can lift his eyes to the stars.   Bernard, before describing the creation of man at the hands of four goddesses, puts into the mouth of one of them a forecast of what the finished product is to be.   Among man's characteristics is that noted by Firmicus:

> Bruta patenter habent tardos animalia sensus,
>   Cernua dejectis vultibus ora ferunt;
> Sed majestatem mentis testante figura,
>   Tollet homo sacrum solus ad astra caput,
> Ut cœli leges indeflexosque meatus
>   Exemplar vitæ possit habere suæ.[2]

seems to have borrowed a part of his attack on Firmicus from Firmicus himself.   In the opening chapters of the *Mathesis,* Firmicus, in fairness to the adversaries of astrology, rehearses some of their arguments before proceeding to refute them, and discusses at some length the contention that astrology subverts laws and morals (cf. *Matheseos Libri VIII:* ed. Kroll and Skutsch, Leipzig, 1897-1913, 1. 6-8).   It is this passage which finds an echo in Marbodus.   The latter presents in general a curious problem for the hunter of sources.   He asks the astrologer, for example, to explain why the astrological influence of Mars does not seem to act among a law-abiding people like the Brahmins, and why the Jews do not change their customs when they leave their native land—illustrations that are identical with those used by the Gnostic Bardesanes (Eusebius, *Præp. Ev.* 6. 11: Migne, *Patr. Gr.* 21. 475); cf. above, p. 20.

[1] See below, p. 61.

[2] Quoted in Cousin's *Ouvrages Inédits d'Abelard* (Paris, 1836), p. 634.

The last lines of this quotation lead the reader to suspect that, for Bernard Silvestris, Firmicus was not only a source of information on matters of astrology, but a seducer as well. A reading of the whole of the *De Mundi Universitate* confirms this suspicion. In the person of Bernard Silvestris, in fact, astrology could boast one of its first mediæval champions. Yet it is not the scientific astrology of Ptolemy and the Arabians that finds expression in his work. It is rather the philosophical astrology of the Neoplatonic commentators, Chalcidius and Macrobius. The second half of the *De Mundi Universitate* is little more than a version of the Timæan myth of the creation of man. The goddess Urania conducts the human soul down to earth by way of the planets, and discourses to her companion-goddesses on the benign influences of some, and the evil powers of others. With a complete abandonment of the orthodox views on the subject, Bernard breaks out into a panegyric of the wonderful science of the stars:

> Præjacet in stellis series quam longior ætas
>   Explicet, et spatiis temporis ordo suis
> Sceptra Phoronei, fratrum discordia Thebis,
>   Flamma Phaëtontis, Deucalionis aquæ,
> In stellis Codri paupertas, copia Crœsi,
>   Incestus Paridis Hippolytique pudor.
> In stellis Priami species, audacia Turni,
>   Sensus Ulixeus, Herculeusque vigor.
> In stellis pugil est Pollux et navita Typhis,
>   Et Cicero rhetor, et geometra Thales.
> In stellis lepidus dictat Maro, Milo figurat,
>   Fulgurat in Latia nobilitate Nero.
> Astra notat Persis, Ægyptus parturit artes,
>   Græcia docta legit, prælia Roma gerit.
> Exemplar specimenque Dei virguncula Christum
>   Parturit, et verum sæcula numen habent.[1]

Bernard Silvestris is a unique figure in the Middle Ages. Though his work was very popular—the passage just quoted

[1] The Benedictine editors of the *Hist. Litt. de la France*, who quote

is the source of a stanza in Chaucer's *Man of Law's Tale*[1]—it in no wise represents the orthodox thought of his century. The *De Mundi Universitate* is almost purely pagan, and might have been written by a humanist of the sixteenth century. Possibly its glorification of astrology already shows the influence of the science of the Moors.[2] Bernard is interesting as the principal representative of Neoplatonic astrology in the Middle Ages. Except for the use made of it by poets like Dante, Neoplatonic astrology was to have no future.

For an expression of the orthodox attitude of the twelfth century toward astrology, one must look to men like Abelard, Hugh of St. Victor, and, best of all, to John of Salisbury. Abelard, the great innovator in mediæval thought, has only a philosophic interest in the science. He discusses it at some length in his *Analytics,* in connection with the problem of free will, his purpose being to disprove the existence of absolute necessity. Belief in fatalism he calls impossible in the face of actual experience and common sense. Even Nature herself could not predict future happenings contingent upon chance. Hence it is surprising that any one should claim for a science like that of astrology the power of prophecy.[3] Hugh of St. Victor's short notice of astrology in the *Didascalicon* repeats the passage

this stanza (12. 270), greet the impiety of the last lines with a cry of horror; see also the edition of the *De Mundi Universitate* by Barach and Wrobel (Innsbruck, 1876), p. 16.

[1] *Man of Law's Tale* 99-105; cf. Skeat's note (Oxford ed. 5. 147).

[2] Cf. the sentiment of the above stanza with the passage quoted below (p. 50) from Adelard of Bath.

[3] *Analytica Priora* III: 'Mirum est quod dicunt per astronomiam quosdam horum quoque futurorum præscios esse. Quod enim naturæ inopinatum est atque incognitum, quo modo per artem naturalem cognosci possit, aut quo modo ex aliqua rei natura certi esse possimus de eo quod naturæ quoque incognitum est?' (Cousin, *Ouvrages Inédits d'Abelard,* Paris, 1836, p. 285.) Abelard, however, seems to have assented to the mediæval view of magic as

of Isidore's *Etymologiæ* which distinguishes between astronomy and astrology. Hugh of St. Victor introduces, however, a modification in the phraseology of Isidore which will bear close scrutiny, inasmuch as it is prophetic of that new attitude which was beginning to seek expression. Isidore, in making a distinction between natural and superstitious astrology, had given to the former a definition practically identical with that of astronomy, reserving for the latter the accusation that it was a diabolic art. In Hugh of St. Victor, though superstitious astrology stands condemned as in Isidore, the definition of natural astrology reads as follows: 'Natural astrology deals with the influence of the stars upon our bodily complexions, which vary according to the state of the celestial sphere, as in health and sickness, good and bad weather, fertility and drought.'[1] To admit the influence of the stars over sickness and health was a concession of great importance. Although implied in certain statements of Isidore and Augustine, it had rarely been so clearly acknowledged. In truth, if this modification is owing to Hugh of St. Victor himself, it marks him as a pioneer in the development of the scholastic doctrine concerning scientific astrology.

For the maturest expression of the orthodox attitude toward astrology in the twelfth century, one must look to John of Salisbury. An Englishman by birth, educated in

possible when carried on by the aid of demons. And with characteristic perversity he even defends the study of necromancy and magic. He inserts a plea for it into his defense of dialectic. Knowledge even of evil serves some good; only the practice is to be condemned. God himself knows what the devil is about (*Analytica Posteriora* I: Cousin, p. 435).

[1] *Didascalicon* 2. 11 (Migne, *Patr. Lat.* 176. 756): 'Astrologia autem quæ astra considerat secundum nativitatis et mortis, et quorumlibet aliorum eventuum observationem, quæ partim naturalis est, partim superstitiosa. Naturalis in complexibus corporum, quæ secundum superiorum contemperantiam variantur, ut sanitas, ægritudo, tempestas, serenitas, fertilitas, et sterilitas.'

France, and living in Paris, Canterbury, and Chartres, John of Salisbury is the best representative of that incipient humanism which had grown up in the school of Chartres, and which was soon to give way before an age of science and theology. The philosophical problems connected with astrology and fatalism had for John of Salisbury a peculiar fascination, and he discusses them at great length in the *Policraticus,* written about 1159. Although John of Salisbury was unusually sane and enlightened in the matter of mediæval superstitions,[1] he subscribed fully to the patristic doctrine of demonology. The Church Fathers, he says, rightly denounced all forms of magic—*species mathematicæ*—inasmuch as all of these pestiferous arts spring from an illicit pact with the devil.[2] The various kinds of divination he defines as does Isidore, reserving the usual place for the *astrologi* and *mathematici.*[3]

But the kinship between astrology and the diabolic arts of divination is little emphasized when John of Salisbury, in the second book of the *Policraticus,* deals with astrology in its philosophical and scientific aspects. He admits at the outset that some power may reside in celestial bodies, since God has created nothing without its proper use.[4] Astronomy, indeed, is a glorious science; only when it bursts its proper bounds does it become impious. A distinction is to be made between the legitimate science—*mathĕsis*—and the illegitimate divinatory art—*mathēsis.*[5]

[1] See particularly his chapters on omens (*Pol.* 2. 1 ff.) and on dreams (2. 14 ff.); cf. Hansen, *Zauberwahn,* p. 128.

[2] *Pol.* 1. 9: 'Eo quod [Patres] omnia hæc artificia vel potius maleficia ex pestifera quadam familiaritate dæmonum et hominum noverint profluxisse' (ed. Webb 1. 49).

[3] *Pol.* 2. 12 (*ibid.* 1. 53). John of Salisbury includes Tertullian's statement that astrology was a permitted science until the time when the Magi worshipped at Bethlehem; see above, p. 18.

[4] *Pol.* 2. 19 (*ibid.* 1. 107).

[5] John of Salisbury probably found this distinction in Hugh of St. Victor (*Didasc.* 24: Migne, *Patr. Lat.* 176. 753). It occurs

The latter, in attempting to foretell the future, usurps the prerogatives of the Creator of the stars himself.[1] John of Salisbury proceeds to make mild fun of the astrologers' doctrines.[2] Departing from the ways of true science, he says, they divide the signs of the zodiac into masculine and feminine, and would probably have the constellations contract marriages in the sky, were they not too far separated in space. Saturn the astrologers characterize as cold and wicked; he spares from harm scarcely the astrologers themselves.[3] John of Salisbury, however, quite forgets his sarcasm in the portion of his exposition where he describes the astrological powers of the sun. If astrology, in fact, were only content with moderate claims, and occupied itself with sober predictions of the weather, all would be well. But when the astrologers make broad their philacteries, and enlarge the borders of their garments in ascribing everything to the stars, they do injury to God's sovereignty.[4] They even teach that feats of magic can be performed by the aid of the stars, and that a human image can be brought to life, gifted with the power of prophecy. With such nefarious arts the Christian can have nothing to do.[5] The doctrine of Plotinus, to be sure, which holds that the stars are used by God himself to give to men signs of future events, is fairly plausible. Are not birds and other things the instruments through which God transmits to men knowledge of what is to come?[6] Still, under the honey of such

also in Roger Bacon (*Opus Majus* 4. 16: ed. Bridges, London, 1900, I. 238).

[1] *Pol.* 2. 19 (ed. Webb I. 108).

[2] *Ibid.* His information seems to come from Firmicus Maternus.

[3] Omnibus ergo inimicus vix suis etiam scolasticis parcit' (*ibid.* I. 108).

[4] *Pol.* 2. 19 (*ibid.* I. 111).

[5] *Ibid.*

[6] *Ibid.* The editor of the *Policraticus* is puzzled as to where John of Salisbury got his information about Plotinus. If one puts together a passage of Macrobius (*Somn. Scip.* I. 19. 8) and one from Augustine (*Civ. Dei* 5. 1), I think there is no need to look further.

a theory poison lurks. For, under pretext of showing reverence to God, the philosophers impose a fatalistic rule upon the course of human events. And fatalism, other than that implied in the doctrine of God's foreknowledge, is as hateful to John of Salisbury as it was to Augustine. He expounds at great length the Church-doctrine concerning predestination and free will[1]; and when he again returns to astrology, it is only to attack it more fiercely than ever with theological arguments. Taking his cue from Abelard, he denies that man can gain any knowledge of the future whatsoever. Has the astrologer obtained access to the secret counsels of God himself?[2] Does not the story of king Hezekiah prove that God can alter even his own prophecies?[3] John of Salisbury does not deny that God may at times indicate future events by the sun and moon; but he is persuaded, on the authority of reason and the concurrent opinions of many other philosophers, that a science foretelling the future either does not exist, or is unknown to men.[4]

Clearly, John of Salisbury's attitude toward astrology is that of the Church Fathers in mediæval dress. Living at a time when Arabian science was already filtering into western Europe by way of Latin translations, he was still oblivious of its presence. His own countryman, Adelard of Bath, had already made a journey of exploration into Saracen lands; and in his own school of Chartres, traces of Arabian astrology can be found in the cosmological writings of William of Conches, who died five years before the *Policraticus* was written.[5] But there are no proofs that John of Salisbury knew Adelard of Bath; and his

[1] *Pol.* 2. 20-24 (*ibid.* 1. 113-33).
[2] *Pol.* 2. 24 (*ibid.* 1. 136).
[3] *Ibid.;* cf. 2 Kings 20. 1.
[4] *Pol.* 2. 25 (*ibid.* 1. 136).
[5] Adelard of Bath and William of Conches will be discussed in a later chapter (see below, pp. 49, 61). The latter died in the year 1154; the *Policraticus* was written 1159-60.

interest in the scientific studies for which the Chartres school of the early half of the century was famous, seems to have been of the slightest.[1] John of Salisbury, in effect, saw in astrology little more than a dangerous philosophical doctrine. He is distinctly at a loss in dealing with it as a science.[2] He would probably have been unable to define exactly where he drew the line between a legitimate science of astrology, useful in predicting the weather, and that impious *mathēsis* which he condemns with rhetoric as forceful as that used by Augustine. His concessions to astrology as a physical science are hardly in advance of those found in the *De Civitate Dei*.[3]

John of Salisbury stands at the close of the first period in the history of mediæval astrology. From the time of Isidore to the middle of the twelfth century, astrology, it may be said, lived only in the form of an academic discussion. Even astrological texts, other than Firmicus Maternus, were unknown to the Latin world. John of Salisbury probably had little more acquaintance with actual astrologers than did Burchard of Worms, or Rabanus Maurus.[4] A century and a half was still to elapse before

[1] This point is made by Schaarschmidt (*Johannes Saresberiensis,* Leipzig, 1862, p. 151). Clerval (*Les Ecoles de Chartres,* p. 317) furnishes proof of the fact that quadrivial studies in the Chartres school no longer occupied in the latter half of the twelfth century the position of prominence which they had held in the first.

[2] It is perhaps significant that John of Salisbury, though he bases his statements largely upon Augustine, does not once make use of the ancient arguments of Carneades.

[3] Some light is shed upon John of Salisbury's attitude toward astrology by his views regarding signs in general. He believes firmly that God makes use of signs to forecast important events (*Pol.* 2. 1-4): 'Infidelitas namque signorum argumentis erigitur, et fides tenera eisdem roboratur.' He gives a long description of the signs that preceded the fall of Jerusalem (*ibid.* 2. 4 ff.), and does not doubt the prophetic virtue of comets (*ibid.* 2. 13).

[4] It is perhaps going too far to say that John of Salisbury had no acquaintance with astrologers, particularly in view of his own state-

the Church burned at the stake its first astrological heretic, and it was still two centuries before Petrarch could hold up to scorn the astrologers of the Milanese court. But already at the time when John of Salisbury was writing his learned defense of free will, the scientific works of Aristotle, and the astrological treatises of Ptolemy and Albumasar, were beginning to find their way into the schools of France and Italy. With their discovery, a new chapter opens in the history of astrology, as in that of mediæval philosophy.

ment to the contrary: 'Plurimos eorum audivi, novi multos, sed neminem in hoc errore diutius fuisse recolo, in quo manus Domini condignam non exercuerit ultionem' (*Pol.* 2. 26: ed. Webb I. 143). But any personal contact he may have had with astrologers has left no other trace in his argument.

CHAPTER III

ASTROLOGY IN OLD ENGLISH LITERATURE

Astrological learning, as we have seen, was almost
extinct in Europe during the Dark Ages; hence we need
not expect to discover more than occasional signs of its
existence in northern vernacular literature. All astrological
science among the Teutonic peoples, indeed, must be termed
a foreign importation—even the popular astrology of the
almanac goes back to Greece and Rome. Certain primitive
superstitions among the Teutons and Gauls, it is true,
offered points of contact for simple astrological notions.
Cæsar, describing the religion of the Germans, says that
they worshipped as gods only those whose power they
could easily recognize, namely the Sun, Vulcan, and the
Moon.[1] Tacitus, in the *Germania,* informs us that the
Teutonic tribes held their assemblies on stated days—'either
at the new or the full moon, which they account the most
auspicious season for beginning any enterprise.'[2] In the
English laws of Cnut, a statute is included which forbids
all heathenish practices, and, incidentally, the worship of
sun or moon.[3] The Penitential of the English archbishop,
Theodore of Canterbury (died 690), furthermore, contains
slight references to superstitions regarding the moon.[4] An

[1] Cæsar, *De Bello Gallico* 6. 21. Students of mythology are puzzled
over this reference; cf. R. M. Meyer, *Altgermanische Religions-
geschichte* (Leipzig, 1910), p. 105.

[2] Tacitus, *Germania,* chap. 11.

[3] Cnut's law reads: 'Hæþenscipe byð þæt man īdola weorðige,
þæt is þæt man weorðige hæðene godas, and sunnan oððe mōnan, fȳr
oððe flōd. . . .' See Liebermann, *Die Gesetze der Angelsachen*
(Halle, 1903) I. 312; or Thorpe, *Ancient Laws and Institutes of
England* (London, 1840), p. 162. Similar to this law of Cnut is a
passage in Ælfric's *Homilies* (ed. Thorpe I. 366).

[4] Theodore, *Liber Pœnitentialis,* chap. 27 (Thorpe, *Anc. Laws,*
p. 292).

entire chapter in this work is devoted to magic and sorcery—
an interesting commentary on the popular beliefs of the
time. Augury from the flight of birds is found in the list
of malpractices,[1] as are also necromancy, and the consulting of witches.[2] Observance of New Year's Day according
to heathen customs is forbidden.[3] Last of all, the archbishop warns against the attempt to stop an eclipse by
means of enchantment, and prescribes a year's penance for
any one 'qui in honore lunæ pro aliqua sanitate jejunat.'[4]

The observance of lucky and unlucky days seems to be
the nearest approach to astrology in the superstitions of
the ancient Celts. Several accounts are on record of Druids
who predicted a child's future according to the day on which
it was born.[5] There also existed among the Druids a form
of cloud-divination, and the corresponding Celtic word,
neladóracht, is at times applied to astrology and divination
in general.[6] Certain puzzling references to astrology proper
which appear in the Christian literature of Ireland—one
passage, for example, relates how a diviner scans the
heavens, and tells the foster-father of St. Columkille that
the time is propitious for his son to begin his lessons—are
hardly sufficient to prove the existence of an indigenous
astrological science.[7]

The pagan worship of sun and moon, and the observance
of lucky and unlucky days, though they cannot yet be called

---

[1] *Liber Pœn.* 27. 7.

[2] *Ibid.* 27. 13, 20.

[3] *Ibid.* 27. 24.

[4] *Ibid.* 27. 25, 26.

[5] Joyce, *Social History of Ancient Ireland* (2 vols., London, 1903)
I. 233.

[6] *Neladóracht* glosses *pyromantia* (divination by fire) in an old
Irish treatise on Latin declension (*ibid.* I. 229).

[7] *Ibid.* I. 230. A more elaborate proof of the fact that the ancient
Druids were ignorant of astrology is given by La Ville de Mirmont.
in *L'Astrologie chez les Gallo-Romains,* pp. 7-20 (*Bibliothèque des
Universités du Midi,* Vol. 7).

astrology, constitute a foundation upon which it can build. Accordingly, we find in Old English a series of treatises, translated from Latin or Greek originals, which appealed to such primitive beliefs. Some of these treatises—a number of them have been printed by Cockayne in his collection of Old English *Leechdoms*[1]—belong to the realm of medicine, and indicate the days in each month which are favorable or unfavorable for the letting of blood.[2] Another consists of meteorological prognostications, according to the day of the week on which Christmas falls. 'If the mass-day of midwinter is a Sunday,' one prophecy reads, 'then there shall be a good winter, and a windy spring, and a dry summer, and good vineyards; and sheep shall thrive, and honey shall be sufficient, and peace shall be kept well enough.'[3] Still another contains miscellaneous predictions for each day of the lunar month. For the thirteenth, the treatise prophesies: 'The thirteenth day is perilous for beginning things. Dispute not this day with thy friends. The fugitive will quickly be discovered. A child born

[1] Cockayne, *Leechdoms, Wortcunning, and Starcraft of Early England* (Rolls Ser.) 3. 150-229.

[2] *Ibid.* 3. 152, 182.

[3] *Ibid.* 3. 162 ff. An article by Max Förster, *Die Kleinliteratur des Aberglaubens im Altenglischen* (*Archiv* 110. 346-58), in discussing these astrological texts, proves that they belong to the learned, not the popular literature of the time. Förster is able to cite the Greek or the Latin sources for most of them. Several Latin parallels are found in Migne's *Patrologia Latina* (90. 951 ff.), ascribed to Bede. The *Prognostica Temporum* (Migne, p. 951) corresponds to the treatise just referred to in Cockayne. The *De Minutione Sanguinis* (Migne, p. 959) furnishes the source for part of an Old English medical text (Cockayne 3. 76). The *De Divinatione Mortis et Vitæ* (Migne, p. 963) is a Latin vulgarization of a famous Greek treatise on divination, dating from the Alexandrian period, current under the name of Nechepso and Petosiris. In its mediæval form, it still preserves much of the Greek terminology. Cf. Sudhoff, *Jatromathematiker, vornehmlich im 15. und 16. Jahrhundert* (*Abhandl. zur Gesch. d. Medizin*, 1902), pp. 6-7.

this day will be plucky, having a mark about his eyes, bold, rapacious, arrogant, self-pleasing, and will not live long. A maiden will have a mark on the back of her neck or on the thigh; she will be saucy, spirited, daring of her body with many men: she will die soon. A man fallen sick on this moon will quickly recover, or be long ill. A dream will be fulfilled within nine days. From the sixth hour it is a good time for blood-letting.'[1]

It is only by courtesy, of course, that compilations like these are allowed to claim kinship with the science of Ptolemy and Manilius. Primitive as they are, they belong to the learned literature of the day, and trace their origin to foreign, not to native, sources. In the course of centuries, this learned superstition became the common property of the uncultured, and the stock in trade of the maker of almanacs. A popular song, found in a manuscript of the fifteenth century, predicting the weather for the year if Christmas falls on a Sunday, exhibits an exact counterpart of one of the texts printed by Cockayne.[2]

The homilies of Ælfric furnish evidence that even the belief in lucky and unlucky days met with the hostility of the English Church. The observance of so-called 'Egyptian days' had been forbidden as early as Augustine,[3] and Ælfric was therefore on orthodox ground when he attacked such popular superstitions in a sermon for New Year's. After exhorting against divination in general, he rebukes those in particular who 'regulate their journeys by the moon, and their acts according to days, and who will not undertake anything on Mondays.'[4]

[1] Cockayne 3. 190.

[2] Denham, *A Collection of Proverbs and Popular Sayings* (Percy Society, 1845), p. 69; cf. Cockayne 3. 162.

[3] *Super Epist. ad Galatos,* chap. 4. This passage was taken up into the Church law; cf. Ivo of Chartres, *Decretum* 9. 15 (Migne, *Patr. Lat.* 161. 750).

[4] Thorpe, *Homilies of Ælfric* (2 vols., London, 1844) 1. 100. A similar denunciation of the belief in unlucky days, as of augury

Probably the only extended reference in Old English to astrology proper is to be found in Ælfric's homily on the Epiphany. Ælfric, following the lead of Gregory, connects with the story of the Magi[1] a discussion of destiny and free will. 'We are also to know,' Ælfric says, 'that there were some heretics who said that every man is born according to the position of the stars, and that by their course his destiny befalls him.' The manner in which Ælfric thus introduces the subject shows clearly how foreign it must have been to his English hearers; the mere use of the past tense is significant. And when he continues with an elaboration of the ancient argument of twins, utilizing Augustine's illustration of Jacob and Esau, his words can have aroused in his hearers little more than a historical interest.[2]

Although England, like the rest of Europe, had to content itself during the early mediæval period with the mere

and witchcraft in general, is found in Ælfric's poetic *Lives of Saints* (No. 17: *EETS*. 82. 370). Ælfric himself was not altogether free from the astrological superstitions of the time. In his vernacular version of Bede's *De Temporibus* (its authenticity is no longer doubted; cf. C. L. White, *Ælfric,* Boston, 1898, p. 124), he subscribes to the belief in the moon's influence over growing things, and in comets (Cockayne 3. 269, 273; cf. Thorpe, *Homilies* 1. 610). One may note, however, that Ælfric's version of Alcuin's *Interrogationes Sigeulfi,* in which Bede is the source for a description of the planets, omits Bede's references to the 'coldness' of Saturn and the 'heat' of Mars (*Anglia* 7. 14-5).

[1] Ælfric translates the Latin *magi* with the Old English *tungolwītigan* (Thorpe 1. 110).

[2] A. Fischer (*Aberglaube unter den Angel-Sachsen,* Meiningen, 1891, p. 22) is surely wrong when he takes this homily, as well as the texts printed by Cockayne, as proof that astrology was 'still' current among the English in the tenth century. In reality, Ælfric's reference is nothing more than a literary allusion. In applying it to the belief in Fate, he had his hearers, of course, directly in mind. Cf. Fischer (p. 21) for references in Old English to Wyrd. See especially Alfred's Boethius 39. 8 (ed. Sedgefield, Oxford, 1899, p. 131).

rudiments of an astrological science, it was destined to play an important rôle in the scientific movement of the later centuries. Even before the days of the new science, there can be found in England traces of that revived interest in astrology which culminated in the *De Mundi Universitate* of Bernard Silvestris, and the philosophical writings of John of Salisbury. A curious story is told by William of Malmesbury, which shows that Firmicus Maternus, discovered on the continent during the eleventh century, must have traveled to England shortly after the Norman Conquest. The chronicle relates how Gerard, Archbishop of York from 1100 to 1108, who was reputed to have meddled with magic, was refused burial by his canons because a copy of Firmicus was found under his pillow at his death.[1] In the first quarter of the twelfth century, we also meet with a reference to astrology in Geoffrey of Monmouth. At the close of the seventh book of the *Historia Regum Britanniæ,* and as a part of the famous prophecies of Merlin, there occur a series of obscure astrological allusions[2]—a passage which puzzled Geoffrey's followers, and did not find an interpreter until the fifteenth century, when the French chronicler Waurin explained it as referring to the day of judgment.[3] Although the prophecy is probably little more than a jumble of classical reminiscences—one of its sources, apparently, was Lucan's *Pharsalia*[4]—it indicates that astrological ideas were already

---

[1] *Gesta Pontificum Anglorum* 3. 18 (ed. Hamilton, Rolls Ser., pp. 259-60). The story is told also by Higden in his *Polychronicon* (ed. Lumby, Rolls Ser., 7. 420).

[2] *Historia Regum Brittaniæ* (ed. Schulz, Halle, 1854), pp. 100-101.

[3] Waurin, *A Collection of the Chronicles and Ancient Histories of Great Britain* 2. 57 (ed. Hardy, Rolls Ser., 1. 250 ff.).

[4] Viktor Rydberg, *Astrologien och Merlin,* Stockholm, 1881. Most of Geoffrey's allusions are only vaguely astrological. Such phrases as 'the amber of Mercury' and 'Stilbon of Arcady' may mean anything or nothing (Stilbon, the Greek name for Mercury, is found in Martianus Capella). The most definite astrological allu-

in the air. Adelard of Bath, indeed, was Geoffrey's own contemporary. With the second quarter of the century, in effect, we are on the threshold of that new age of mediæval science which was to honor astrology as the chief of the seven arts, and to make of astrologers the confidants of popes and kings.

sions occur in his references to the 'malignity of Saturn' and the houses of the planets. Two other slight references to astrology occur in Geoffrey's *Historia*. In the first (9. 12), it is stated that many astronomers lived at Arthur's court. The second passage (12. 4) relates at greater length how, in the reign of king Edwin, a Spaniard, Pelletus, came to the English court, and employed the arts of astrology and augury to guard the realm from foreign invasions. Both Wace and Layamon follow Geoffrey in these two notices.

CHAPTER IV

ARABIAN ASTROLOGY

Little is known of the life of Adelard of Bath, the pioneer student of Arabic science and philosophy in the twelfth century, and 'the greatest name in English science before Robert Grosseteste and Roger Bacon.'[1] Born in England, probably before 1100, he traveled in the East as far as Syria, and, on his return, occupied himself with making the astronomy and geometry of the Arabs available to the Latin world. In addition to several independent works, there can be ascribed to him with confidence a treatise on the astrolabe, translations of Euclid's *Elements* and of the astronomical tables of Mohammed ben Musa al-Khuwarizmi, and, in particular, a version of the *Isagoge Minor* of Albumasar, one of the standard text-books of Arabian astrology.[2]

One of the earliest of Adelard's independent works, the *De Eodem et Diverso*,[3] concerns itself principally with a description of the seven liberal arts, figured successively as seven virgins. Astronomy closes the procession. 'She appears, surrounded by a shining splendor, her body all eyes. In her right hand she holds a quadrant, in her left, an astrolabe. Her science describes the whole form of the world, the courses of the planets, the number and size of

---

[1] Wright, *Biographia Britannica Literaria* (London, 1842-6) 2. 94.

[2] Haskins, *Adelard of Bath (Engl. Hist. Rev. 26. 491-7).* Cf. Wüstenfeld, *Die Übersetzungen Arabischer Werke in das Lateinische (Abhandlungen der Gesellschaft der Wissenschaften zu Göttingen 22. 21)*, and Suter, *Die Mathematiker und Astronomen der Araber (Abhandlungen zur Geschichte der Mathematik 10. 11)*, two works which in general supplement the chapters on the translations out of Arabic into Latin of Jourdain's *Recherches Critiques sur l'Age et l'Origine des Traductions Latines d'Aristote* (Paris, 1843, pp. 97 ff.).

[3] Written, it may be, as early as 1109 (Haskins, p. 492).

their orbits, the position of the signs; she traces parallels and colures, and measures with sure hand the twelve divisions of the zodiac; she is ignorant neither of the magnitude of the stars, nor of the position of the poles, nor of the extension of the axes. If a man acquire this science of astronomy, he will obtain knowledge, not only of the present condition of the world, but of the past and future as well. For the beings of the superior world, endowed with divine souls, are the principle and cause of the inferior world here below.'[1] Such was to be the naïve faith of the new age in the science of the stars! Astrology and astronomy, so carefully confined to separate compartments by Isidore of Seville, were again united. For several centuries, the latter was destined to be the mere servant of the former.

The *De Eodem et Diverso* gives evidence that Adelard of Bath was connected in some way with the school of Chartres[2]; it was among its students that Adelard's voyage of discovery into the Orient found its first imitators. Peter the Venerable, Abbot of Cluny, while traveling in Spain in 1141, met Herman of Dalmatia, a pupil of Thierry of Chartres, and Robert of Retines, an Englishman, both engaged in the study of astronomy (astrology).[3] Peter the Venerable persuaded them to turn aside for a time from their main pursuit, and to make a Latin version of the Koran. But in 1143 they were again occupied with their astrological translations. Among the several fruits of their labors, not the least in importance was the version made by Herman of the *Introductorium in Astronomiam* of Albumasar.[4] No other astrological text-book, as we shall see, did

---

[1] *Des Adelard von Bath De Eodem et Diverso. Zum ersten Male herausgegeben und historisch-kritisch untersucht von Dr. Hans Willner*, Münster, 1903 (in Bäumker's *Beiträge* 4. 1. 31-2).

[2] See Duhem, *Le Système du Monde* 3. 169.

[3] Clerval, *Les Ecoles de Chartres*, p. 189.

[4] Duhem 3. 174.

more to make astrology acceptable to the Church of the succeeding century.

At about the same time that Herman of Dalmatia and his friend Robert were devoting themselves to the translation of astrological texts in Spain, others were engaged in the same task. By the middle of the twelfth century, in fact, most of the important works on astrology had found their way into Latin. In 1138 Plato of Tivoli translated Ptolemy's *Tetrabiblos* (henceforth to be known by its Latin name as the *Quadripartitum*).[1] Not much later appeared a version by John of Seville (also known as Johannus Hispanus, or Lunensis) of the famous *Centiloquium*—a series of one hundred astrological aphorisms falsely attributed to Ptolemy. To John of Seville are also due versions of Albumasar's *Liber Conjunctionum Siderum* and *Flores Astrologiæ,* as well as astrological texts of the Arabian, Alchabitius, and the Jew, Messahala.[2] The prince of translators appeared finally in the person of Gerard of Cremona (1114-87), to whom some seventy translations from the Arabic can be ascribed. Among these were the famous versions of Ptolemy's *Almagest,* and of two hitherto unknown works of Aristotle, which play an important rôle in the history of astrology—the *Meteorologica* and the *De Generatione et Corruptione.*[3]

What, it may be asked, was the nature of this new astrology, which, like the new Aristotle, had been made accessible to Latin readers in the space of a few decades? To answer this question, it is necessary to glance at the history of Arabian astrology in general—a history which it is difficult to trace. Astrology had been introduced into the Mohammedan world in the eighth century, at the time when Caliph Al-Mansur, calling to his aid the learned Jew, Jacob

[1] Wüstenfeld, p. 40.
[2] *Ibid.,* pp. 25 ff.
[3] *Ibid.,* p. 67.

ben Tarik, founded at Bagdad a school for the mathematical
sciences. It was in this school that, in the ninth century,
the greatest of Arabian astrologers, Albumasar, received
his training. From its introduction, down to the time when
the West became acquainted with it in the Saracen schools
of Toledo and Cordova, astrology won the allegiance of a
host of Arabic and Jewish scientists. Among the noted
astronomers whose names appear in the Latin literature of
the Middle Ages, were Messahala, Albategnius, Alpetragius,
Alchabitius, and Abenragel.[1]

Arabo-Judæan astrology was a jumble of systems and
doctrines. The Jewish scholars who introduced it into the
Moorish schools were versed, not only in the pure astrology
of Ptolemy, but also in that of other Greek masters, such as
Vettius Valens, Dorotheus Sidoneus, Teucer, and Antiochus,
who themselves had amalgamated the most diverse theories.[2]
This Greek astrology, furthermore, had been contaminated
with the demonology and magic of the *Talmud,* and the
mysticism of the *Cabala.*[3] Throughout the Middle Ages,

---

[1] *Jewish Encyclopædia 2. 244; Catholic Encyclopædia 2. 21.*

[2] *Encyclopædia of Islam* 1. 495 (article *Astrology,* by C. A.
Nallino).

[2] The *Book of Enoch* (R. H. Charles and W. R. Morfill, *The Book
of the Secrets of Enoch,* tr. from the Slavonic, Oxford, 1896),
appearing about the time of the Christian era, is the best evidence
that astrological doctrines had early found their way into Jewish
circles. Even St. Paul's reference (1 Cor. 12. 2-4) to his being
carried to the seventh heaven is a reminiscence of this work
(Bouché-Leclercq, p. 607). From the time of the *Book of Enoch*
to the appearance, in the thirteenth century, of the great Cabalistic
text, the *Zohar,* the influence of astrology upon Jewish mysticism
was on the increase (see *Jew. Enc.* 3. 456; 2. 244; Pick, *The
Cabala,* Chicago, 1913). The magic of Cornelius Agrippa, and
of the Jews of the later centuries, can be conveniently studied in
the German translation published at Stuttgart in 1855 (Heinrich
Cornelius Agrippa, *Magische Werke,* 5 vols.). The Jewish treatise
of Arbatel (5. 95 ff.) is characteristic. The seven planets are
identified with seven master-spirits, and directions are given for

astrology constituted an integral part of the necromancy and divination of Jews and Moors alike—a relationship which proved embarrassing when astrology tried to win converts in Christian lands, where intercourse with demons was not tolerated.[1] Fortunately, this contaminated astrology was left largely to the practitioners of necromancy and magic proper. The standard astrological text-books, written usually by astronomers, remained free from it.

But the scientific treatises of Albumasar, Abenragel, and Alchabitius present a marked contrast to the classic astrology which we have already encountered. The *Tetrabiblos* of Ptolemy had confined itself almost exclusively to judicial astrology—the prediction of the future according to the configuration of the stars at birth. In the astrological texts of the Arabians, judicial astrology occupied a position of distinctly minor importance. Its place was taken by two other systems, current at the time of Ptolemy, which he had deliberately ignored—the so-called *interrogationes* and *electiones*. The system of *interrogationes*, as its name implies, consisted of a series of rules by means of which the astrol-

the utilization of their powers (5. 111 ff.). Arbatel distinguishes between good and evil spirits, and maintains throughout an orthodox tone. Cf. above, p. 17.

[1] Belief in the power of *jinns* was not forbidden by Islam (*Encyclopædia of Religion and Ethics* 4. 818). This accounts for the fact that the black arts flourished in Moslem countries as much as did pure astrology. The two were taught side by side in the famous schools of Toledo and Cordova (J. W. Brown, *Life and Legend of Michael Scot,* Edinburgh, 1897, p. 187). Few text-books of Arabian magic and necromancy have been preserved, since the ecclesiastical censorship of the Middle Ages dealt with them much more severely than with astrological treatises. The *Encyclopædia of Religion and Ethics* (4. 817) gives an account of one treatise on magic, the famous *Goal of the Sage* of the eleventh century, and Brown's *Life and Legend of Michael Scot* (pp. 183 ff.) discusses in some detail the magic of mediæval Spain. Notes on many books concerning magic now lost are found in the *Speculum Astronomiæ,* ascribed to Albert the Great (ed. Jammy, 1751, 5. 656-66)).

oger answered questions regarding the discovery of a thief, a lost treasure, the trustworthiness of a friend, or the wealth of a prospective bride.[1] The system of *electiones,* on the other hand, determined the propitious moment for undertaking any act of daily life. The rules of this system, too, were elaborated in great detail, even to the extent of naming the proper time for the cutting of finger-nails, the writing of a letter, or the boarding of a ship.[2] The system of *electiones* was particularly favorable to the development of medical astrology, and was in general merely a scientific elaboration of the common belief in lucky and unlucky

[1] An excellent example of the system of *interrogationes* is furnished by the astrological work of Abenragel, the most complete of the Arabic texts which were translated into Latin (the copy in the Yale Library is entitled: *Præclarissimus Liber Completus in Judiciis Astrorum, quem editit Albohazen Haly Filius Abenragel,* Venice, 1485). The first half of this work, consisting in all of eight books, and numbering some three hundred pages in the Latin translation, is devoted to answering such minute questions as those enumerated above (see fols. 14[b], 28[b], 55[b]). Abenragel lived from 1116-52, and therefore comes at a period when Arabian astrology had been fully developed. His work was not translated until 1256 (cf. Suter, p. 100), and did not influence Western writers as did the treatises of Albumasar. His text, however, furnishes better opportunities for study than the much shorter *Introductorium* of Albumasar (New York Public Library) or the *Isagoge* of Alchabitius (Columbia University Library).

[2] Abenragel, fols. 113[a], 116[a]. Many Arabian astrologers adopted, as part of the *electiones,* the Indian system of twenty-eight lunar mansions, which afforded an opportunity for more minute calculations than that of the twelve houses (Abenragel, fols. 126[a] ff.; cf. *Enc. of Islam* 1. 496). This system of lunar mansions could easily serve for magical purposes, and seems to have been in bad odor with Church writers. In the *Speculum Astronomiæ,* ascribed to Albert the Great, the twenty-eight lunar mansions are expressly connected with diabolic arts (*Alberti Magni Opera,* ed. Jammy, 1751, 5. 656). The clerk of Chaucer's *Franklin's Tale* employs these lunar mansions. See Tatlock's article in *Kittredge Anniversary Papers,* Boston, 1913, p. 348.

days.[1] In truth, the system of *electiones* enjoyed a distinct superiority over the rival doctrines of judicial astrology. Confining itself to a definition of favorable or unfavorable conditions, and not attempting to predict the future itself, it avoided the fatalism which was an inevitable element in the astrology of Ptolemy. As a part of medical astrology, it had little difficulty in finding a welcome at the hands of the Christian scientists of the thirteenth century.

On its philosophical, no less than on its practical side, astrology received modifications at the hands of the Arabians which facilitated its acceptance by Christian theologians. Concomitant with the introduction of Ptolemy into the Mohammedan world had been that of the scientific works of Aristotle; and the cosmology of the *Meteorologica* and *De Generatione et Corruptione* had, in course of time, formed an inseparable part of astrological theory. When Aristotle, therefore, became for the Latin scholars the 'master of those that know,' it was inevitable that astrology should likewise meet with a friendly reception.

One of the first astrological treatises to be carried north from Spain, as we have seen, was the translation of Albumasar's *Introductorium in Astronomiam*, made by Herman of Dalmatia. No work was better suited to bring to the knowledge of the Christian schools the philosophical principles of Arabian astrology.

Albumasar, after dividing the science of the stars into its two main divisions, undertakes, in the second chapter, a defense of astrology. He begins by enunciating the Aristotelian doctrine of the fifth essence: The substance of the astral bodies does not consist of one of the four elements of this world, nor of a combination of these elements. If it were formed of the elements of this world, it would suffer growth and decay, dissolution, and the other

---

[1] Bouché-Leclercq, pp. 458 ff. The system of *electiones* was logically incompatible with judicial astrology. Ptolemy accordingly made no place for it in his system.

changes to which earthly things are subject. Since all this is foreign to the celestial world, one must conclude that the substance of the stars consists of a certain fifth essence. The stars are spherical bodies, transparent, and endowed with a perpetual motion. This motion of the stars is circular, the one motion which is perfect and eternal.[1]

Circular motion is found also in the sublunary sphere. It is circular motion that is seen in the processes of growth and decay—in the concomitant generation of one substance and the destruction of another substance. Now this process of growth and decay is a cyclic motion, which decomposes one substance, and transmutes it into another substance, changing the latter, in turn, back into the former. Its cause is none other than the eternal circular motion of the stars. The motion of the upper sphere acts upon the world below, and brings about that mingling of element with element which is necessary for all generation and corruption. Hence the Philosopher declared[2] that the inferior world was in some necessary way bound up with the superior world, so that the sphere of the stars, in revolving with a natural motion, carried with it the world below. But generation and corruption are at the foundation of all motion and change on earth. One may conclude, therefore, that the celestial essence exerts an influence on everything that takes place on the mundane sphere.[3]

Aristotle, in affirming the dependence of the lower upon the upper spheres, had drawn a distinction between the uniform motion of the fixed stars and the irregular motion of the planets, and had made of the first the principle of

[1] *Introductorium in Astronomiam Albumasaris Abalachi, octo Continens Libros Partiales*, Augsburg, 1489 (copy in New York Public Library), unpaged, bk. 1, chap. 2: sig. a5ᵇ.
[2] *Met.* 1. 2 (see above, p. 3).
[3] *Introductorium*, sig. a6ᵃ.

permanence, and of the second the principle of change.[1] Albumasar formulates a similar doctrine as follows: All that is born and dies on earth depends upon the motion of the constellations and of the stars. . . . Now the seven wandering planets march along the zodiac more swiftly than do the constellations, often changing from direct to retrograde. They are, therefore, better adapted than the upper sphere to produce the effects and the motions of the things of this world. To the sphere of the constellations is assigned a general rule; whereas to the wandering stars belongs the care over the details of earthly life. . . . The more rapidly a planet moves, and the stranger the course which it follows, the more powerful will be its influence on things below. The motion of the moon is swifter than that of any other planet; it has, accordingly, more to do than any other in regulating mundane affairs. The fixed stars govern what is stable in the world, or what suffers gradual change. The celestial sphere of the fixed stars encircles the earth with a perpetual motion; the stars never alter their pace, and maintain invariable their relative distances from the earth. The seven planets, on the contrary, move more rapidly and with diverse motions, each running its own variable course. . . . As the motions of these wandering stars are never interrupted, so the generations and alterations of earthly things never have an end. Only by observing the great diversity of planetary motions .can one comprehend the unnumbered varieties of change in this world.[2]

The *Introductorium in Astronomiam,* in undertaking a general defense of astrology, touches also upon the philosophical question involved in astrological fatalism. It is

---

[1] *De Gen. et Cor.* 2. 10 (see above, p. 3).

[2] *Introductorium,* bk. 3, chap. 1 (ed. in New York Public Library, sig. b7[b]). Albumasar elsewhere (1. 2: sig. a6[a]) gives an outline also of Plotinus' doctrines, according to which the stars are only indicators of future events; cf. Duhem 2. 372-3. See above, p. 2.

worth while to listen with care to Albumasar's solution of
the problem. The *Introductorium in Astronomiam* already
points the way to that compromise between Christianity and
astrology which we shall soon meet in the writings of Albert
and Thomas Aquinas.

Some there are, says Albumasar, who solve the problem
of astrological fatalism by denying the existence of contingent actions altogether, admitting only the necessary and
the impossible. But so complete a denial of freedom runs
counter to the evidence of experience. Contingent things
can be proved to exist. The statement of a necessary fact
holds good for the future as for the past or the present.
We know that fire burns, that it has burned, and that it
will burn; that fire is not cold, that it never was cold, that
it never will be cold. Contingent facts admit of no such
prediction. We know that a man is writing or has written,
but we do not know whether he will or will not write in
the future. The contingent can be proved to exist, moreover, by the fact that we deliberate about it. No deliberation ever takes place concerning the necessary or the
impossible.[1]

A disproof of fatalism, however, does not involve a denial
of stellar influence over contingent things. Albumasar proceeds to show that the power of the stars is seen in the
realms both of the necessary and of the contingent.

The process by which the elements, and the bodies which
they compose, resolve one into the other, the growth and
diminution which even human bodies undergo, come under
the rule of the necessary. Since it is certain that the stars
govern the alterations of sublunary bodies, it is seen that
all necessary things are dominated by the celestial sphere.

Now man is composed of a reasoning soul and an elemental body. The reasoning soul exercises its powers in
deliberation and choice; it rules over the body, and the

[1] Cf. Aristotle's *De Interpretatione,* chap. I.

latter serves to carry out the soul's commands. The stars have also, according to the teachings of the Philosopher, a reasoning soul and a natural motion, and consequently possess the power to modify the harmony existing between man's body and his soul. Hence the power of the stars directs contingent acts, as well as those which fall within the realm of the necessary.[1]

The theory of Albumasar at this point is not easy to understand, and is at best not clear. The leaning toward a deterministic science, indeed, noticeable throughout the treatise, was as little to the liking of the Church as the fatalistic philosophy of the Arabs in general.[2] But the linking up of astrological theory with Aristotelian cosmology, and the specious reasonings on the subject of contingent actions, could not fail to prove alluring to Christian scientists. The *Introductorium ad Astronomiam* served as one of the agents of compromise between the Church and the new astrology of the Moors.

---

[1] *Introductorium,* sig. a8^b ff. The Latin in this portion of the treatise is very difficult. I have been guided by the paraphrase given by Duhem (2. 375-6).

[2] It is doctrines such as those of Albumasar concerning the stellar souls that are repeatedly inveighed against in the edict against heresy published by the University of Paris in 1277. See Denifle-Chatelain, *Chartularium Universitatis Parisiensis* (Paris, 1889) 1. 543 ff. The stellar souls are referred to in the passage quoted above (p. 50) from Adelard of Bath.

CHAPTER V

THE MEDIÆVAL ACCEPTANCE OF ASTROLOGY

By the middle of the twelfth century, practically the entire range of Greek and Arabian science had been thrown open to the Latin world. The appropriation of this treasure was a slow process. The Christian scholars of the twelfth century were too much occupied with the quarrel between realism and nominalism to interest themselves in problems of Aristotelian cosmology.[1] We have seen that John of Salisbury was quite oblivious of the new learning which had already crossed the borders of Spain. Not until the thirteenth century did the science of Aristotle acquire that position of prominence which it was destined to maintain throughout the remainder of the mediæval era.

The first signs of the new interest in Arabian astrology may be found in the school of Chartres, that centre of learning with which Adelard of Bath had formed connection, and which had sent out the first explorers into Mohammedan Spain. Evidence for this fact is found in a list— given by Clerval[2]—of the astronomical books in possession of the Chartres school after Herman of Dalmatia and his fellow-adventurers had returned. Among the number appear several works of Adelard of Bath, and a treatise on judicial astrology by Alchabitius, translated by John of Seville. Traces of Arabian astrology can also be found in the writings of William of Conches,[3] a member of the school of Chartres in the middle of the century.

In the volume of Migne's *Patrologia Latina* devoted to the writings of Honorius of Autun appear two treatises on mediæval cosmology, of neither of which Honorius of Autun is the author. The first, entitled *De Philosophia*

[1] Jourdain, *Recherches*, pp. 227-8.
[2] *Les Ecoles de Chartres*, p. 239.
[3] See above, pp. 33, 39.

Mundi, is a work of William of Conches; the second, entitled *De Imagine Mundi,* that of an obscure Honorius Inclusus, who lived about the year 1100.[1] The *De Imagine Mundi* is a typical encyclopædia of the early mediæval centuries, like those of Bede and Rabanus Maurus, containing naïve descriptions of the planets and the constellations, with no mention of their astrological significance. It affords an excellent contrast to the later work of William of Conches, in which traces of the new science are plentiful. Saturn is here described as cold, and Jupiter as temperate; Mars is *nociva,* and the indicator of war and bloodshed.[2] Venus is the goddess of luxury, 'quia confert calorem et humorem, et in calidis et humidis viget luxuria.' In William of Conches we even find a curious inversion of the Isidorean definition of astronomy and astrology—an inversion which reappears in Roger Bacon, and which certainly can be traced to an Arabian source.[3] As typical representatives of what he calls *astronomia*—the science which, according to his inverted definition, deals with stellar influences—William of Conches names Firmicus Maternus and Ptolemy.[4]

One of the first mediæval Latin writers to mention an

[1] Migne, *Patr. Lat.* 172. 42-102, 122-88. The *De Imagine Mundi* is the principal source for the vernacular *L'Image du Monde* of Gautier of Metz (ca. 1247), one of the most popular encyclopædias of the later mediæval centuries. On Honorius Inclusus, see Duhem 3. 24 ff.; on William of Conches, Duhem 3. 87 ff.

[2] Migne, *Patr. Lat.* 172. 63: 'In prœliis dicitur dominari, quia calorem confert et siccitatem, ex quibus est animositas. Calidi enim et sicci animosi sunt.'

[3] Vincent of Beauvais (*Speculum Doctrinale* 17. 46), after quoting the definitions of astronomy and astrology according to Isidore, also gives them inversely—that is, defining *astrologia* as astronomy, and *astronomia* as astrology—quoting as source for the latter definition the Arabian, Alphorabius. Cf. Roger Bacon, *Opus Majus* (ed. Bridges I. LVIII).

[4] Migne, *Patr. Lat.* 172. 59.

Arabian astrologer by name was Alanus de Insulis. In a description of the seven liberal arts, which constitutes a portion of that curious poetical compendium of knowledge entitled the *Anticlaudianus,* astronomy is no longer differentiated from astrology. Alanus names Albumasar as one of the representatives of the double science[1]:

> Illic astra, polos, cœlum, septemque planetas
> Consulit Albumasar, terrisque reportat eorum
> Consilium, terras armans, firmansque caduca
> Contra cœlestes iras, superumque furorem.

Alanus de Insulis, the mediæval *Doctor Universalis,* belongs to the close of the twelfth century. One of his contemporaries was the Englishman, Alexander Neckam, the author of a prose treatise, the *De Naturis Rerum.* The belief in the astrological influence of the planets and constellations had, by the time of Alexander Neckam, already become a fixed part of scientific doctrine. But Neckam still considers it necessary to safeguard his orthodoxy by means of a caveat. 'Let it not be supposed,' he says, 'that the planets decide things here below by any inevitable law of necessity, either by their conjunctions, or by their being in this or that domicile. For the divine will is the unalterable and primal cause of things, to which not only the planets show obedience, but also created nature as a whole. It must be understood that, although superior bodies have some influence over inferior ones, yet the *arbitrium animæ* is free, and is not impelled by necessity either this way or that.' It is possible that Alexander Neckam is paraphrasing the *Introductorium in Astronomiam* of Albumasar.[2] The discussion of astrology in the *De Naturis Rerum* is cer-

---

[1] *Anticlaudianus* 4. 1 (Migne, *Patr. Lat.* 210. 521).

[2] *De Naturis Rerum* 1. 8 (ed. Wright, Rolls Ser., pp. 39-40). Alexander Neckam's allegorizing tendencies get the better of him even in his dealings with astrology. He identifies the astrological influences of the several planets with the seven gifts of the Holy Spirit—wisdom, intellect, counsel, bravery, science, piety, and fear (pp. 41-2).

tainly one of the earliest attempts to bring the new science of the stars into conformity with Christian thought. Alexander Neckam clearly points the way to the scholastic definition of orthodox astrology formulated in the thirteenth century.

The deciding factor in the development of the scholastic doctrine on the subject of astrology was Aristotle himself. The complete Aristotelian canon had been made accessible in Latin translations between the years 1210 and 1225.[1] Although the treatises on natural science were proscribed several times by Church councils and papal legates, they were gradually purged of the noxious doctrines with which they had become tainted while in the hands of Neoplatonic and Arabian commentators, and by 1255 were accepted as a part of the standard curriculum of the University at Paris.[2] Albert the Great already refers to Aristotle as the 'regula veritatis, in qua natura summam intellectus humani perfectionem demonstravit.'[3]

This general acceptance of Aristotle as the arbiter of human knowledge could not fail to augur well for astrology. No scholastic theologian dared any longer question the Peripatetic teaching that the processes of earthly growth and change depended for their existence upon the stellar spheres. Aristotle's doctrine of the Prime Mover, endowing the heavens with a motion which they in turn impart to the lower spheres and to the earthly elements, fitted easily into a Christian scheme of the universe. Although differing considerably in detail,[4] all of the mediæval interpreters of Aristotle, from Avicenna[5] and Averroes[6] to Albert the

---

[1] Überweg, *Geschichte der Philosophie* (Berlin, 1915) 2. 408.

[2] *Ibid.* 2. 410.

[3] *De Anima* 3. 2. 3.

[4] The various cosmological systems are studied in Duhem's *Le Système du Monde;* see, in particular, 3. 342, 351; 4. 226, 233, 494.

[5] Carra de Vaux, *Avicenne* (Paris, 1900), pp. 251 ff.

[6] *Commentum in De Generatione et Corruptione* 2. 10 (*Aristotelis*

Great,[1] Bartholomæus Anglicus,[2] Thomas Aquinas,[3] and Dante,[4] accepted the Aristotelian theory of motion as a fundamental postulate. And astrological theory had, since the days of Ptolemy, become so inseparable a part of Aristotelian cosmology that the Christian theologians, in welcoming the one, were inevitably compelled to offer a favorable reception to the other.

A modification of such importance in the traditional doctrine of the Church could not take place without a struggle. Since the days of Isidore and Augustine, the *mathematici* and readers of horoscopes had been branded as servants of the devil, and their fatalistic philosophy had been denounced with fiery rhetoric. The casting of nativities had, in fact, been defined as a superstitious art as late as the *Summa Theologiæ* of Alexander of Hales (1245).[5] The scholastic writers of the thirteenth century themselves subscribed to the teachings of the Fathers on the subject of demons and magic.[6] In effecting a compromise, therefore, between the verdict of the early Church and the new astrology, Albert the Great and Thomas Aquinas faced a problem of no slight difficulty.

The theologians of the thirteenth century discovered the clue for its solution in that passage of the *De Civitate Dei*[7]

Opera, ed. 1550, 5. 174); Horten, *Die Metaphysik des Averroes* (Halle, 1912), p. 173.

[1] *De Generatione et Corruptione* 2. 3. 4 (ed. Jammy 2. 65); *Metaphysicorum* 11. 2. 25 (ed. Jammy 3. 389-90), *De Cælo et Mundo* 2. 3. 5 (ed. Jammy 2. 113); cf. Werner, *Die Kosmologie des Roger Baco* (Vienna, 1879), p. 52.

[2] *De Proprietatibus Rerum* 8. 1 ff. (*Batman uppon Bartholome,* London, 1582, fol. 121ᵃ).

[3] *De Cælo et Mundo* 2. 12. 18, 19 (*Opera Omnia,* Rome, 1888-1906, 3. 194, 198); *Summa Theologiæ* 1. 1. 115. 3 (*ibid.* 5. 542).

[4] *Il Convito* 2. 15.

[5] *Summa Universæ Theologiæ,* Quæstio 166. 2 (ed. 1622, 2. 751).

[6] Hansen, *Zauberwahn,* pp. 156 ff.

[7] *Civ. Dei* 5. 6 (Migne, *Patr. Lat.* 41. 146); cf. above, p. 24.

in which Augustine had admitted the existence of an influence of the stars over human bodies, and had demanded merely that the freedom of the human will should be maintained inviolate. Medical astrology, as well as the Arabian system of *electiones,* easily squared itself with this doctrine. The judicial astrology of Ptolemy, even, with its careful distinction between general and individual predictions, and its denial of Stoic fatalism, might have had little to fear at the hands of Augustine himself. The defense of astrology, furthermore, found in Albumasar's *Introductorium,* offering as a substitute for a vulgar divinatory art a reasoned science, based on simple cosmological principles, disarmed even the most orthodox. Theologians were so occupied in combating the outspoken determinism of Arabian philosophy that they were more than willing to compromise on all but the essential issues. The Church, accordingly, accepted astrology as a science, at the same time saving appearances with the patristic doctrine by reasserting its hostility to magic, and condemning judicial astrology whenever it adhered to fatalistic theories, or assumed the rôle of an arbitrary art of divination.

The *Speculum Naturale* of Vincent of Beauvais cites Albert the Great as the source of a series of chapters which define the influence of the stars upon nature and man.[1] A compromise between the cosmology of Aristotle and judicial astrology is here seen to be clearly in the making. Albert, quoting from Augustine's *De Civitate Dei,*[2] takes for granted that the stars govern the material elements. The *anima vegetabilis* of plants and the *anima sensibilis* of animals, inasmuch as they are immediately dependent upon matter, also stand under this necessary rule of the heavens.

---

[1] *Speculum Naturale* 4. 34 ff. (ed. in New York Public Library, fol. 64ᵇ). I have as yet been unable to find, in the works of Albert the Great himself, the passage quoted by Vincent.

[2] *Ibid.,* fol. 65ᵃ.

The human soul, on the other hand, is dependent upon elemental matter not directly, but *secundum quod*. A gathering of blood about the heart, for example, inclines the soul to wrath, but anger is not a necessary consequence. Hence the stars govern the soul's actions only indirectly and not *simpliciter*. They can influence the human will, but only by way of the body.[1] Albert cites in support of his defense of free will the same passage of Aristotle's *De Interpretatione*[2] which Albumasar had employed in a similar connection; and he makes it clear, by means of references to the Fathers, that he does not wish to be accused of leanings toward fatalism.

Albert the Great's concessions to judicial astrology, guarded though they were, sufficed to change the traditional hostility of the Church into an attitude of tolerance. Concrete evidence for this is furnished by Albert's own commentary on the second chapter of Matthew, that story of the Magi which had served so many of the Fathers as a text for a sermon against the astrologers. Albert, in defining the meaning of the word *magus*,[3] takes occasion to discuss the magic arts in general. When he comes to the *mathematici*, he divides them into two groups, according as they represent the pure science of mathematics (*mathĕsis*), or the more dubious practical art of astrology

---

[1] *Ibid.*, fol. 64[b]: 'Sic ergo, secundum quod animus hominis inclinatur, et dependet ad naturam et complexionem, sic etiam habet in eo vim constellatio, videlicet secundum quod et non simpliciter. . . . Quod autem superiorum corporum virtus imponat necessitatem libero arbitrio, etiam contra philosophum est ponere, nisi per hunc modum: quo dicimus inclinari et mutari hominis animum.'

[2] See above, p. 58.

[3] This definition itself sounds strange to ears accustomed to patristic exegesis: 'Magus proprie nisi magnus est, quia scientiam habens de omnibus ex necessariis, et effectibus naturarum conjecturans, aliquando mirabilia naturæ præostendit et educit' (ed. Jammy 9. 24).

(*mathēsis*).[1] On the latter he has this to say: 'If anyone prognosticates by the stars concerning those things only which are subject to natural causes, . . . and to that primal order of nature which exists in the configuration of the stars and heavenly circles, he does not commit a fault, but rather serves a useful purpose, and saves many things from harm. He, however, who predicts the future arbitrarily (*non consideratis omnibus*), and concerning future things other than those defined above, is a deceiver, and is to be shunned.'[2] Underneath this carefully worded definition, one can feel a real enthusiasm for the science of Ptolemy and Albumasar.

Thomas Aquinas, in crystallizing, finally, the orthodox attitude toward astrology of the later mediæval centuries, follows the lead of Albert the Great. Like his predecessor, he accepts the cosmology of Aristotle,[3] and finds equal comfort in the passage of Augustine which admits a rule of the stars over corporeal bodies. He does not hesitate to declare that the employment of astrology for meteorological purposes, and in medicine, is entirely legitimate.[4] As with Albert, the real debate centred in judicial astrology; and Thomas Aquinas, like his predecessor, begins the discussion with a psychological analysis. The human intellect

[1] This distinction, it will be remembered, is found in John of Salisbury. See above, p. 37.

[2] Ed. Jammy 9. 24.

[3] *Summa Theologiæ* 1. 1. 115. 3 (*Opera Omnia,* ed. Rome, 5. 542).

[4] *De Judiciis Astrorum* (*Opuscula Omnia,* Paris, 1634), p. 392: 'Et ideo si aliquis iudiciis astrorum utatur ad prænoscendum corporales effectus, puta tempestatem, et serenitatem aëris, sanitatem vel infirmitatem corporis, vel ubertatem et sterilitatem frugum, et similia, quæ ex corporalibus et naturalibus causis dependent, nullum videtur esse peccatum. Nam omnes homines circa tales effectus aliqua observatione utuntur corporum cœlestium, sicut agricolæ seminant et metunt certo tempore. . . . Medici circa ægritudines criticos dies observant, qui determinantur secundum cursum solis et lunæ;' cf. *Summa* 2. 2. 95. 5 (9. 319).

and will, he says, are not corporeal; consequently they escape that influence which the stars necessarily exert over matter. Indirectly, however, and by accident, the influence of the heavenly bodies does affect intellect and will, inasmuch as both intellect and will are intimately connected with corporeal organs. The intellect, in truth, is necessarily affected whenever man's physical processes are disturbed. The will, on the other hand, does not follow of necessity the inclination of inferior appetite, although the irascible and the concupiscent in man incline the will toward this or that choice.[1] 'The majority of men, in fact, are governed by their passions, which are dependent upon bodily appetites; in these the influence of the stars is clearly felt. Few indeed are the wise who are capable of resisting their animal instincts. Astrologers, consequently, are able to foretell the truth in the majority of cases, especially when they undertake general predictions. In particular predictions, they do not attain certainty, for nothing prevents a man from resisting the dictates of his lower faculties. Wherefore the astrologers themselves are wont to say "that the wise man rules the stars," forasmuch, namely, as he rules his own passions.'[2]

But Thomas Aquinas is not prepared to set aside entirely the patristic teaching that astrology is a diabolic art of divination. He accepts judicial astrology so long as it can prove itself a part of natural science, and he goes just as far as he dares in freeing it from the restrictions with which it had become encumbered in earlier Church doctrine. Nevertheless, there was still remaining a narrow margin of astrological theory which could not be brought within the pale of a reasoned cosmological science. This portion

---

[1] *Summa* I. I. 115. 4, Respondeo (5. 544).

[2] *Summa* I. I. 115. 4, Ad Tertium (5. 544). The phrase 'sapiens homo dominatur astris' recurs many times in the astrological literature of the thirteenth and fourteenth centuries (see below, pp. 135 ff.).

of judicial astrology Thomas Aquinas condemns in the language of the Church Fathers. 'If any one,' he says, 'employs the observation of the stars for predicting fortuitous events, or such as happen by chance, or even for predicting with certainty (*per certitudinem*) a man's future actions, he does so falsely. In this sort of prophecy the activity of demons is called into play.'[1] As for astrological magic, this finds no place in Thomas Aquinas' system. Necromancers, he admits, invoke demons according to the configurations of the stars, but not by reason of any compulsion which the heavens exercise over the fallen angels. The demons come, when thus called, in order to lead men into a belief in the divine power of the stars, and because under certain constellations corporeal matter is better disposed for the result for which they are summoned.[2] Astrological images and charms, such as are employed in medicine, are also under the care of demons. As a proof of this, Thomas Aquinas cites the fact that such images are never efficacious unless inscriptions are written on them, which tacitly invoke the aid of evil spirits.[3]

The long warfare of science with theology, carried on from the days of Tertullian and Augustine, had resulted in a distinct victory for science. Astrology had successfully

[1] *Summa* 2. 2. 95. 5 (9. 320).

[2] *Summa* 1. 1. 115. 4, Ad Secundum (5. 544). Thomas Aquinas firmly believes in the possibility of magic and necromancy.

[3] *Summa* 2. 2. 96. 2 (9. 332). Thomas Aquinas here begs the real question at issue. Other scientists—Roger Bacon, for example (see Brewer, *Opera Quædam Hactenus Inedita,* Rolls Ser., p. 531)—did not take it for granted that inscriptions were necessary for astrological images. It is also interesting to see the Renaissance commentator of Aquinas, Cajetan (his commentary accompanies the text in the Leonine edition), take issue with his master on this point. He cites certain marvelous stories of Guido Bonatti and other astrologers to prove that if images are made at certain hours, they can be used to produce feats of magic without the intervention of demons.

divested itself of the stigma of illegitimacy which it had borne for centuries. Although condemnations of judicial astrology continued to appear in later writers, they were usually in the nature of belated borrowings from Augustine and Isidore. The definition of Thomas Aquinas also left room for differences of opinion in particular cases. It might have been possible to level against almost any professional astrologer the accusation that he was indulging in predictions *per certitudinem,* but the burden of proof would have been laid upon the accuser. As a matter of fact, after the middle of the thirteenth century a sane science had no longer anything to fear at the hands of the Church. Indiscriminate denunciations, such as had found their way into the canon law of Ivo and Gratian, ceased to appear. An indication of orthodox opinion in the last quarter of the century is furnished by a list of proscribed works on the occult arts, which formed a part of a decree against heresy issued in 1277 by Bishop Tempier of Paris.[1] A work on geomancy—a form of divination by means of figures drawn haphazardly by the questioner, and interpreted astrologically—is singled out for condemnation, and a general prohibition is made of all books dealing with the invocation of demons. The decree also takes issue with certain Averroistic doctrines denying the freedom of the will.[2] But a sober astrology is not attacked. A similar pronouncement on superstitious arts, made a century later (1398) by the same University of Paris, is equally lenient.[3] It

---

[1] Denifle-Chatelain, *Chartularium Universitatis Parisiensis* (Paris, 1889) 1. 543 ff.

[2] No. 162. 'Quod voluntas nostra subjacet potestati corporum celestium.'

No. 207. 'Quod, in hora generationis hominis in corpore suo et per consequens in anima, que sequitur corpus, ex ordine causarum superiorum et inferiorum inest homini dispositio inclinans ad tales actiones vel eventus.—Error nisi intelligatur de eventibus naturalibus, et per viam dispositionis.'

[3] *Ibid.* 4. 32 ff.

denounces the use of magic in all forms, even for good purposes, and terms it blasphemous to believe that there are good demons as well as bad, and that the former can be enclosed by magic rites in stones or vestments, and thus made to serve man. It even calls 'true astrology' to witness that it is contrary to natural science to believe in images of brass or wax, which, when consecrated on certain days, posses marvelous virtues.[1] Astrology itself is inveighed against only when it teaches that the actions of the human intellect and will are under the necessary governance of the stars.[2]

In truth, the demands made on judicial astrology by Thomas Aquinas, instead of being condemnatory of its fundamental principles, were rather suggestions for improvement similar to those which scientists were themselves advocating. The best instances of this fact are furnished by the writings of Aquinas' own contemporary, Roger Bacon. England, during the early part of the thirteenth century, had begun to assume a position of prominence in European science. Robert Grosseteste, Bacon's own master, and a leader at the new University of Oxford, already shows an enlightened interest in astrology. Grosseteste's writings on the subject would have been exactly to the liking of Thomas Aquinas. He gives a full outline of astrological theory regarding the influences of the planets and constellations,[3] urging the employment of astrology

---

[1] 'Quod ymagines de ere vel de plumbo vel auro vel de cera alba vel rubea vel alia materia baptizate, exorcizate, et consecrate seu potius execrate secundum prædictas artes et sub certis diebus habeant virtutes mirabiles, que in libris talium artium recitantur. Error in fide, in philosophia naturali, et astrologia vera' (*ibid.* 4. 35).

[2] 'Quod cogitationes nostre intellectuales et volitiones interiores immediate causentur a celo, et quod per aliquam traditionem magicam tales possunt sciri, et quod per illam de eis certitudinaliter judicare sit licitum. Error' (*ibid.*).

[3] *De Impressionibus Aëris seu de Prognosticatione* (Baur, *Die Philosophischen Werke des Robert Grosseteste*, Münster, 1912, pp. 41 ff.).

for meteorological predictions, and in chemistry, medicine, and agriculture.[1]   He also discourses at length upon the astrological significance of comets.[2]   But of judicial astrology he says not a word.   Roger Bacon, like his predecessor, sees in the new astrology something more than a divinatory art.   He says expressly that even if judicial astrology were abolished altogether, enough would be left to constitute a science of immense value.[3]   All the great masters from Aristotle[4] to Albumasar, he asserts, repudiated its vulgar practitioners, especially those who contaminated it with necromancy.[5]   In the matter of judicial astrology, Ptolemy himself made a distinction between general and particular prognostications.   Only in the former can certainty be attained.   In predicting the future, the true astrologer does not prophesy necessary events, but merely indicates motives and tendencies.[6]   Prognostications of particular human actions, to be sure, often prove successful, since character and morals depend largely on bodily health.   General predictions, he suggests, can be of great service to the Church itself.   He cites as an example of a legitimate prophecy the horoscopes of the various religions of the world, instituted

[1] *De Artibus Liberalibus* (Baur, pp. 5 ff.).   Grosseteste enumerates three practical uses of astronomy (astrology) : 'vegetabilium plantatio, mineralium transmutatio, ægritudinum curatio.'

[2] *De Cometis* (Baur, pp. 36 ff.).

[3] *Opus Majus, Pars Quarta* (ed. Bridges, London, 1900, I. 248).

[4] Bacon assumed that Aristotle was the author of the *Secretum Secretorum* (ibid. I. 246).

[5] *Ibid.* I. 240.   The *Speculum Astronomiæ*, ascribed to Albert the Great, but probably written by Bacon (see below, p. 102), says that many books of magic try to assume a scientific air by clothing themselves in astrological language: 'Scintillationis gratia, sibi mittunt quasdam observationes astronomicas, ut sic se reddant aliquatenus fide dignos' (*Alberti Magni Opera*, ed. Jammy 5. 658).

[6] *Opus Majus* I. 249, 252.   Bacon asserts that it was only fatalistic astrology that had been reprehended by the Church Fathers, and cites passages to prove that they accepted the true science (I. 246).

by Albumasar.[1] According to the latter, a major conjunction of Jupiter with one of the other planets signified the rise of a new religion. The conjunction of Jupiter with Saturn had brought about the Hebrew religion; that with Mars, the Chaldean; that with the Sun, the Egyptian; that with Venus, the Mohammedan; and that with Mercury the Christian. The conjunction with the Moon, signifying the religion of Antichrist, was still in prospect. According to Bacon's slightly unorthodox chronology, the Mohammedan religion would soon have completed its course—a hope for which he finds additional warrant in the mystic numbers of the Apocalypse. He therefore breaks out into a panegyric on the wonderful science which thus corroborates the Christian faith, and predicts the overthrow of its enemies: 'Propter quod laudandus est Deus, qui philosophis dedit lumen sapientiæ, per quod lex veritatis confirmatur et roboratur, et per quod percipimus inimicos fidei destrui debere.' Roger Bacon, indeed, exhausts his eloquence in praise of astrology, emphasizing above all its utility in medicine.[2]

Roger Bacon probably overstepped the bounds of conservative opinion on the subject of judicial astrology only in the enthusiasm with which he applied it to sacred

---

[1] *Ibid.* 1. 253-66.

[2] *Ibid.* 1. 266. The editor of the *Opus Majus* (Bridges 1. 269) comments on Bacon's belief in astrology in a passage that is worthy of quotation: 'To a believer in a limited and spherical universe, with a terrestrial centre, nothing could seem more valid as a working hypothesis for explaining physical changes on the earth's surface than that alterations of the directions in which the planets were seen should be followed by corresponding alterations of terrestrial objects. The combinations of planetary bodies, as seen in conjunction, in opposition, or in intermediate positions, offered a wide field of speculation, which became practically boundless when to the apparent relation of these bodies to one another were added their apparent relations (also ever varying) with the fixed stars. Human and terrestrial events, complicated as they might be, were

things.[1] In the matter of astrological magic, he undoubtedly progressed beyond the limits set by Thomas Aquinas. Bacon condemns magic by the aid of demons, holding the view that most of it is fraud anyway[2]; but magic that simply utilizes the marvelous influences of the stars finds in him an enthusiastic supporter. Images and verbal charms, if made under the proper constellations, are endowed with unusual powers, because they store up the mysterious energy of the stars and of the human spirit.[3] Bacon quotes in all earnestness a story, told by Josephus, in which Moses escapes from a compromising love-affair with an Ethiopian princess by giving her a ring causing forgetfulness.[4] Many of the miracles of saints, he says, were performed by means of magic words, spoken at the proper astrological moment.[5] In his *Speculum Astronomiæ*,[6] and his *Epistola de Secretis Naturæ*,[7] he even ventures to

paralleled by equal complication in the play of celestial forces. It may be said, on the whole, that so far from belief in astrology being a reproach to Bacon and his contemporaries, to have disbelieved in it would have been in the thirteenth century a sign of intellectual weakness. It conformed to the first law of Comte's *philosophia prima* as being the best hypothesis of which the ascertained phenomena admitted.'

[1] He almost undertakes, in one passage, to write the horoscope of Christ himself (*ibid.* 1. 267).

[2] Brewer, *Opera Inedita,* p. 523.

[3] *Opus Majus* 1. 395-7.

[4] *Ibid.* 1. 392.

[5] *Ibid.* 1. 395.

[6] A work until recently ascribed to Albert the Great. Mandonnet, in an article in the *Revue Néo-Scolastique* (17. 313-35), has fairly proved—to the satisfaction of so recent a scholar as Duhem (3. 216), at least—that it was written by Roger Bacon, probably shortly after Bishop Tempier of Paris had issued his decree against books on magic and geomancy. The *Speculum* is found in the *Opera* of Albert the Great (ed. Jammy 5. 656 ff.); in part, also, in *Catalogus Codicum Astrologorum Græcorum* (Brussels, 1898-1906) 5. 85 ff. Cf. above, p. 53.

[7] Brewer, p. 532.

defend certain condemned books on magic, maintaining that some of them are merely thought to be bad, but really contain useful scientific facts. In books on geomancy, especially, he sees no harm, since he finds that this divinatory art employs scientific methods—'confidit Saturno et domino horæ.'[1] In utterances like these Bacon was certainly indiscreet. Geomancy was among the arts of divination upon which the Church permitted no compromise.[2] It is possible that Bacon's own imprisonment, at the hands of the Minister General of the Franciscan order, followed as a direct result of the publication of the *Speculum Astronomiæ*.[3]

The Church, fearing perhaps that it had dealt too leniently with astrology in theory, gave evidence that it could be all the more severe with it whenever in practice it meddled with magic or with fatalistic doctrines. It was ostensibly on these two accounts, at any rate, that the Inquisition condemned to the stake its first astrological heretic, Cecco d'Ascoli, professor of astrology at the University of Bologna in the first quarter of the fourteenth century. The author of an encyclopædic poem, the *Acerba,* of an astronomical commentary on the *Sphæra* of Sacro-Bosco, and of several minor astrological texts, Cecco d'Ascoli has in recent years aroused much historical interest.[4] His execution at Florence, in 1327, following upon

---

[1] *Spec. Astr.,* chap. 16 (ed. Jammy 5. 660).

[2] Aquinas, *Summa* 2. 2. 96. 3.

[3] Mandonnet, p. 334.

[4] According to Soldati (*La Poesia Astrologica nel Quattrocento,* Florence, 1906, p. 65), whose judgment of the controversial literature on the subject is recent and mature, the best of the many biographies of Cecco is that of Bariola, *Cecco d'Ascoli e l'Acerba,* Florence, 1879. Two excellent short articles are those by Boffito: *Perchè fu Condannato al Fuoco l'Astrologo Cecco d'Ascoli* (*Studi e Doc. di. Stor. e Diritto* 20. 366 ff.), and *Il 'De Principiis Astrologiæ' di Cecco d'Ascoli* (*Giorn. Stor. di Lett. It.,* Suppl. 6). I have

a previous condemnation of his teachings at Bologna, and involving the usual amount of Italian intrigue, is still something of a mystery. According to Giovanni Villani, our best authority, he was found guilty by the Franciscan inquisitor of three heretical doctrines: First, that in the aerial spheres there existed malign spirits which could be constrained, by means of enchantments performed under certain constellations, to perform many marvelous things. Secondly, that he had ascribed a necessary influence to the heavens. Thirdly, that Christ's birth, poverty, and death had been according to the rule of the stars.[1] There can be no doubt that Cecco was guilty on the first count—that of having had dealings with the necromancy of the Jews and Moors.[2] He is, in fact, an excellent representative of that scientific magic which was spreading over Europe from the Orient, and which was making its first important home in Italy. The second and third counts upon which Cecco stood accused are more difficult to substantiate. His works contain a liberal sprinkling of pious phrases and a long discussion of Ptolemy's theory of free will.[3] Cecco is careful to quote the application of astrology to Christ

not seen the biography of Cecco by G. Castelli (Bologna, 1892), nor the recent edition of the *Acerba* by P. Rosario (Lanciano, 1916).

[1] Giovanni Villani, *Croniche* 10. 40 (ed. Florence, 1823, 5. 55-6). A similar astrological interpretation of the life of Christ is found in a work of the Italian lawyer, Lignano (died 1383); see Fantuzzi, *Notizie degli Scrittori Bolognesi* (Bologna, 1796) 5. 39. Cf. also the article on Lignano by Professor A. S. Cook, *Rom. Rev.* 8. 371.

[2] Boffito, *Perchè fu Condannato,* p. 375; Bariola, p. 9. In the *Acerba* is found a small manual of the black arts (4. 4: ed. Venice, 1820, p. 203; cf. Gower, *Conf. Am.* 6. 1261 ff.), which closes with the advice to the listener that he should prove their efficacy for himself. Passages in his prose works are frequent which show that Cecco not only believed in the possibility of diabolic magic—a thing which the Church never denied—but advocated its practice.

[3] See the philosophical defense of astrology in his prose commentary of the *De Principiis Astrologiæ* of Alchabitius (*Giorn. Stor.,* Suppl. 6, p. 4).

at second hand.[1] But the general tone of his writings, even as we have them, can be legitimately suspected of heresy. Astrology was assuming in Italy a much bolder tone than in the universities of France and England. Cecco d'Ascoli came, too, at a time when the Church, under the guidance of Pope John XXII, was unusually energetic in its persecution of magical practices.[2] Cecco d'Ascoli has frequently been ranked very high as a scientist. He himself presumably believed in his own teachings, and the story goes that he preserved at his trial and execution a magnificent calm.

Cecco d'Ascoli atoned for the sins of many; his death forms an almost isolated instance in the history of the Inquisition. The boldness of his utterances, his lack of official patronage, and the fact that he was exposed to the calumny of powerful rivals, subjected him to dangers from which lesser and greater men were exempt. Italy, in fact, during the course of the thirteenth century had become the great European centre of astrology outside of Mohammedan Spain. At the universities of Bologna, Padua, and Milan, the list of professors of astrology is continuous from the early thirteenth to the sixteenth century, boasting the names of such famous scientists as Pietro d'Abano, Giorgio Peurbach, and Regiomontanus.[3] Bologna is credited with the possession of a chair of astrology as early as 1125.[4] At the courts of Emperor Frederick II and Eccelino da Romano, Moorish and Jewish astrologers

---

[1] Boffito, *Perchè fu Condannato*, p. 380.

[2] See the several papal letters which Pope John XXII wrote on the subject of magic between the years 1313 and 1331, published in J. Hansen's *Quellen und Untersuchungen zur Geschichte des Hexenwahns und der Hexenverfolgung* (Bonn, 1901), pp. 2-7.

[3] Gabotto, *L'Astrologia nel Quattrocento* (*Riv. di Fil. Scient.* 8. 378 ff.).

[4] Burckhardt, *Die Kultur der Renaissance in Italien* (10th ed., Leipzig, 1908) 2. 240.

practised the most mercenary of arts. In the service of the former was a certain Theodorus, and Michael Scot, the translator of Averroes. Besides some astrological texts, Michael Scot furnished the emperor with a work on physiognomy,[1] and he is also known as the author of a treatise on geomancy.[2] Whatever be the final verdict on this man as a philosopher or scientist, he was famed in his time as a vulgar magician,[3] and Boccaccio calls him 'gran mæstro in nigromanzia.'[4] Frederick's contemporary, Eccelino—so the chronicles tell us[5]—surrounded himself with a host of necromancers, astrologers, and magicians: 'Master Salio, a canon from Padua, Riprandino of Verona, Guido Bonatti, and Paul, a Saracen with a white beard, who came from Baldach in the remote Orient, and who, by reason of his origin, aspect, and actions, deserved the name of a second Balaam.'

Perhaps the most famous professional astrologer of the thirteenth century was Guido Bonatti. Although in the intellectual and social scale he stood above most of his fellow-craftsmen—he is the author of one of the popular mediæval text-books on astrology—his science, nevertheless, would hardly have met with full approval on the part of Thomas Aquinas. As an example of the kind of ser-vices he rendered his masters, Filippo Villani[6] relates that while in the employ of Guido de Montefeltro, he would mount the campanile to observe the stars at the outbreak of any military expedition. At the first striking of the bell, the count and his men would put on their armor; at the

[1] Wüstenfeld, p. 100.

[2] J. W. Brown, *Life and Legend of Michael Scot* (Edinburgh, 1897), p. 190.

[3] See Scartazzini, *Divina Commedia* (Leipzig, 1874) 1. 220.

[4] *Decam.* 8. 9.

[5] Muratori, *Rer. Ital. Script.* 8. 705, 344; 14. 930.

[6] Quoted by Boncompagni, in *Della Vita e delle Opere di Guido Bonatti* (Rome, 1851), p. 6.

second stroke, they would mount their horses; and at the third, spur their steeds to a gallop. Experience testifies, says Villani, that by this means the count won many a victory.

That Guido Bonatti was credited with having dealt with magic, one can readily understand.[1] Even more contrary to the orthodox opinion of the time, however, was his philosophical defense of the science. In his *Astronomiæ Tractatus Decem,* he virtually denies Ptolemy's distinction between general and particular predictions, as well as the Christian doctrine of free will. 'All things,' says Guido Bonatti, 'are known to the astrologer. All that has taken place in the past, all that will happen in the future—everything is revealed to him, since he knows the effects of the heavenly motions which have been, those which are, and those which will be, and since he knows at what time they will act, and what effects they ought to produce.[2] A passage like this shows why the scholastic theologians insisted upon reservations before accepting the science of the Moors.

Guido Bonatti did not, like his successor Cecco d'Ascoli, pay for his heresy at the stake. But he met a condemnation, in the eyes of later centuries no less effectual, at the hands of Dante. As the poet and his guide descend to the fourth chasm of the eighth circle, they meet a people coming silent and weeping. The face of each is turned to the loins—'because he wished to see too far before him, he now looks behind and goes backward.'[3] Among the last, Virgil points out two of Dante's countrymen:

[1] Boncompagni, p. 6.

[2] *Decem Continens Tractatus Astronomie* I. 3 (copy in Boston Public Library), Venice, 1506, sig. a2^b. The treatise is prefaced, to be sure, by a pious address to God and the Virgin. The thirteenth chapter of the first book (sig. a5^b) attempts to prove that the Church Fathers, and even Christ himself, employed astrology.

[3] *Inf.* 20. 38-9.

Quell altro, che ne' fianchi è così poco,
    Michele Scotto fu, che veramente
    delle magiche frode seppe il gioco.
    Vedi Guido Bonatti . . .[1]

But Dante, condemning astrology in the *Inferno* in so far as it is a diabolic art, restores it to its proper place in Christian cosmology and ethics in the *Purgatorio* and *Paradiso*. For Dante, the influence of the stars upon human life was indeed an awe-inspiring fact. The heavens are the instruments of God.[2] It is to them that the First Mover has delegated the power to mould the destinies of the world[3]; they are the hammers, earth the metal[4]; they are the seals, and earth the wax.[5] Were it not for the influences of the stars, children would be exactly like their parents. Dante, in effect, reverses the Augustinian argument concerning twins, by pointing to the heavens as the only possible cause of Jacob's differing from Esau.[6] The Platonic myth of the *Timæus* is employed in the symbolism which assigns the saints to their different spheres.[7] His own arrival in the constellation Gemini he explains on the ground that it rules over his nativity.[8] Can Grande's noble character is due to the fact that he was stamped at his birth by the strong star of Mars.[9] According to Brunetto

---

[1] *Ibid.* 20. 115-8: 'That other who is so small about the flanks was Michael Scot; and of a truth he knew the play of magic frauds. See Guido Bonatti—.'

[2] *De Monarchia* 2. 2: 'Instrumentum eius [Dei], quod cœlum est.'

[3] *De Mon.* 2. 2; 3. 2; 3. 16; *Ep.* 5. 133-5; *Par.* 2. 121; 8. 97-9; *Conv.* 3. 15. 159-61.

[4] *Par.* 2. 127-9.

[5] *Par.* 2. 130-2; 13. 73-5; 8. 127; 1. 41, 42.

[6] *Par.* 8. 130-5.

[7] This symbolism is not rigorously carried through. The fact that the unfaithful are in the moon has no astrological significance.

[8] *Par.* 22. 112 ff.

[9] *Par.* 17. 76-8.

Latini's advice to the poet, obedience to one's horoscope becomes a positive duty.[1] The ethical problem involved in the belief in an astrological cosmology, Dante solves as does Thomas Aquinas. Marco's speech to the poet in the sixteenth canto of the *Purgatorio*[2] might be regarded as the final expression of the orthodox doctrine concerning astrology:

> Voi che vivete ogni cagion recate
> pur suso al ciel, così come se tutto
> movesse seco di necessitate.
>
> Se così fosse, in voi fora distrutto
> libero arbitrio, e non fora giustizia
> per ben letizia, e per male aver lutto.
>
> Lo cielo i vostri movimenti inizia;
> non dico tutti: ma, posto ch'io il dica,
> lume v' è dato a bene ed a malizia,
>
> E libero voler, che, se fatica
> nelle prime battaglie col ciel dura,
> poi vince tutto, se ben si nutrica.
>
> A maggior forza ed a miglior natura
> liberi soggiacete, e quella cria
> la mente in voi, che il ciel non ha in sua cura.
>
> Però, se il mondo presente disvia,
> in voi è la cagione, in voi si cheggia,
> ed io te ne sarò or vera spia.

Dante's condemnation of the astrologers and diviners in the twentieth canto of the *Inferno* indicates as yet no disbelief in the efficacy of their art, though in the case of

---

[1] *Inf.* 15. 55. M. A. Orr, in *Dante and the Early Astronomers* (London, 1914), points out that Dante nowhere mentions such details of practical astrology as the houses or aspects of planets, or the division of signs into masculine and feminine, mobile and stable. See this work for a full list of Dante's references to astrology.

[2] *Purg.* 16. 67-84 (ed. Moore, Oxford, 1892, p. 75).

Michael Scot some scepticism is implied when he is accused of 'magic frauds.' The crime of the diviners was one of impiety, not charlatanism. Since the time of the Church Fathers, in fact, the practitioners of divination had not been refuted with rationalistic arguments. It was enough for Dante and Thomas Aquinas, as for Augustine and Tertullian, that magic was wicked; after deciding that it was wrong, logic had done its duty.[1] With rare exceptions the writers of the Middle Ages took astrology, even in the vulgar manifestations which it classed with necromancy, quite seriously. It was not because it might be less successful that Thomas Aquinas condemned astrological prediction *per certitudinem,* but because it had to do with demons. Benvenuto da Imola expresses the mediæval view when he gives as a reason for the truth of Michael Scot's prophecies the very fact that he mingled necromancy with astrology.[2]

It remained for the arrival of the modern spirit, and especially of its first great representative, Petrarch, to join to the scorn shown to the necromancer by mediæval piety the laughter of the satirist. Petrarch, living at the court of the Visconti at Milan, had, indeed, an excellent opportunity to observe the professional astrologers at their worst. The astrologer-necromancer of the time was an ignorant fellow, who knew little of his own science, and nothing of astronomy proper, who employed simple tables for his calculations, and who would have been quite unable to discourse on the philosophical problems involved in his profession.[3] Petrarch, who was in general quick to see

[1] Tatlock (*The Scene of the Franklin's Tale Visited,* Chaucer Soc., 1914, p. 34) characterizes the Middle Ages similarly.

[2] *Commentum* (Florence, 1887) 2. 88: 'Et nota quod Michael Scottus admiscuit nigromantiam astrologiæ; ideo creditus est dicere multa vera.'

[3] Soldati, in *La Poesia Astrologica nel Quattrocento* (pp. 109 ff.), gives a good characterization of the astrologers of the fourteenth

through the pretenses of the pseudo-learned,[1] makes sport of his fellow-courtiers. In a letter on the subject of astrology, written to Boccaccio in the year 1363, he relates a number of amusing stories regarding them.[2] Galeazzo II, consulting his astrologers on the occasion of a campaign against Pavia, held back his army for many days in order to await the favorable astrological moment. When he was finally permitted to march out, the weather, which had been dry during the time of waiting, turned suddenly, and a fierce rain spoiled the whole expedition.[3] The astrologers suffered another discomfiture in connection with the installation into office, in 1354, of the three sons of Giovanni Visconti. Petrarch himself had been asked to deliver an oration, but was interrupted by the astrologers, who were awaiting the exact point of time at which the stars would be most propitious. When this had finally

and fifteenth centuries; and Gabotto's charming essay, *L'Astrologia nel Quattrocento* (referred to on p. 77), cites historical documents illustrating their charlatanry. Cf. also Burckhardt, *Die Kultur der Renaissance in Italien* 2. 238 ff.

[1] Petrarch's treatment of physicians is especially illustrative of his attitude toward astrologers. The medicine of his day was hateful to Petrarch, because it was founded upon the writings of the Arabs, for whose literature and science he had as much disdain as for its unchristian philosophy, exemplified in Averroes (cf. *Seniles* 12. 1, 2: ed. 1581, pp. 905, 913). Petrarch wrote an entire treatise, the *Contra Medicos*, against the physicians of his time, in which he indulges in virulent satire of their quackeries (*op. cit.*, pp. 1091, 1093, 1100). He admits that the science itself is possible, at least in the mind of God, but that in its present form it is a fraud (*Sen.* 12. 2: *ibid.*, p. 906). He even obtained a confession from a physician 'quod medicinæ notitia delectabilis est, ut reliquarum omnium quæ arte et regula continentur; operari autem secundum medicinam *a casu* est. I tu, nunc,' he says to his friend Donatus, 'et casui fidem habe!' (*Sen.* 5. 5: *ibid.*, p. 801.) Cf. Henschel, *Petrarca's Urtheil über die Medicin und die Ärzte seiner Zeit* (Janus, *Zeitschr. für Gesch. und Lit. der Med.* 1. 183-223).

[2] *Sen.* 3. 1 (*ibid.*, pp. 765 ff.).

[3] *Ibid.*, p. 769.

arrived, the astrologers presented the three brothers successively with a sceptre, but paused so long with the first two that when they finally approached the third, the original happy configuration of the stars must have long since gone by. A year, however, had not passed, says Petrarch, before Matteo Visconti, the eldest of the three, the one who had received the sceptre at the favorable astrological moment, lost his rule, and, shortly after, his life. The other two lived in prosperity ten years longer.[1] Petrarch, in a conversation with one of the astrologers of the Milanese court, obtained from him the confession that his art was vain, but that the necessity of supporting his family forced him to continue the fraud.[2]

Strange to say, when Petrarch turns from satire to dialectic, and attempts to refute astrology in theory, he no longer employs rationalistic arguments, but the ancient theological rhetoric of Augustine.[3] Petrarch's attack on astrology as a whole is divided between satirical comment on the quacks who lead the populace by the nose, and fierce denunciation of the astrologer's impiety. Like John of Salisbury, he asserts that the future is known to the Creator alone. Astrology would shift the blame for wrong-doing upon God himself. 'Why,' he asks the astrologer, 'do you thus make weary heaven and earth, and vex mankind in vain? Why do you burden the lucid stars with your empty laws? Why do you turn us, who were born free, into slaves of the insensible stellar spheres?'[4] And he sums up his advice to Boccaccio in the words: 'Close your eyes to tricksters, and your ears to magicians;

[1] *Ibid.*

[2] *Ibid.* Pio Rajna (*Giorn. Stor.* 10. 104 ff.) identifies this astrologer with Mayno de Mayneri, who is known to have lived at the court of the Visconti at this time.

[3] *Fam.* 3. 8 (pp. 611 ff.); *De Remed. utr. Fortun.* 1. 112 (pp. 94-6).

[4] *Sen.* 1. 7 (p. 749).

shun physicians, flee astrologers; those destroy your life, these your soul.'[1]

Petrarch seems to have known little of the astrological science of his own day. As representatives of astrology he does not name the Arabian masters, nor the more modern authorities, but Firmicus Maternus and Ptolemy.[2] He does not attack astrology as a cosmological science, nor does he take notice of the scholastic teachings on the subject. He admits, in passing, that there may be some power in the constellations, and advises the astrologers to predict the weather.[3] As a poet, too, he frequently subscribes to astrological doctrines.[4] In a letter to Emperor Charles he mentions with pride a prediction that he would be upon terms of intimacy with almost all of the great princes of his age.[5] Petrarch even has to admit that he is not altogether free from the popular astrological superstition regarding the climacteric years, nine and seven. On the occasion of his sixty-third birthday (a multiple of the two unlucky numbers), he writes to Boccaccio,[6] scorning such puerile beliefs. A year later, however, referring to the same subject, he confesses that he wrote the former letter more to strengthen the faith of his friend than because he himself was entirely without apprehension. A curious insight into the mind of this great humanist is afforded

[1] *Sen.* 3. 1 (p. 770): 'Claude oculos præstigiis, aures magis, vitam medicis, astrologos fuge: illi corpora, hi animos lædunt.'

[2] *Sen.* 1. 7. (p. 748).

[3] *Sen.* 3. 1. (p. 767).

[4] *Rime* 7. 5-6 (ed. Carducci e Ferrari, p. 9):

> Et è sí spento ogni benigno lume
> Del ciel, per cui s'informa umana vita.

Cf. *Rime* 4. 4 (p. 6), in which he describes the configuration of the stars at the birth of his mistress; and 128. 52 (p. 197), where he attributes the sad state of Italy to a malignant star.

[5] *Fam.* 23. 2 (tr. Fracassetti 5. 10).

[6] *Sen.* 8. 1 (ed. 1581, p. 829: tr. Fracassetti 1. 442).

by his statement to Boccaccio: 'To say the truth, the security which I expressed in my former letter sprang, not so much from a feeling of scorn for the threats of the astrologers, as from a desire to continue my meditations on the necessity of death and the folly of fearing it.'[1]

Petrarch's attitude toward astrology—on the one hand reminiscent of the conservatism of the early mediæval centuries, and, on the other, pointing ahead to the time when astrology would be universally laughed to scorn— was founded, in the first instance, upon indifference to science as a whole.[2] In his own and in succeeding centuries, his religious abhorrence of astrology was shared by numerous philosophers and theologians. His own friend, Coluccio Salutati, although paying some respect to the scholastic cosmology of Thomas Aquinas, follows Petrarch in denouncing astrology as an empty science and a vain art.[3] He even rehearses some of the ancient arguments of Carneades, such as that concerning twins.[4] Gerard Groote, the Dutch reformer of the fourteenth century, condemns the entire science of astronomy, as one that is hostile to God and to the teachings of Augustine.[5] This revival of the

---

[1] *Sen.* 8. 8 (ed. 1581, p. 843: tr. Fracassetti 1. 494).

[2] Petrarch's attitude toward medicine is again illustrative.

[3] A. Martin, *Mittelalterliche Welt- und Lebensanschauung* (Munich and Berlin, 1913), pp. 105-18.

[4] Martin, pp. 112-3; cf. above, pp. 11, 20, 46.

[5] Groote is writing to dissuade a friend from bringing out a book which would refute the heresies of Albumasar, and substitute a true astronomy. Groote argues that the whole science is so bad that it had best be left alone altogether: 'Ad ejus igitur destructionem plus proficit quod falsi sunt libri quam quod accuratæ veritati appropinquarent. Quid mihi profuit magis, creditis, vel Albumasaris et similium error, vel palliata frons Ptolemæi ad astronomiam dimittendam?' (Acquoy, *Gerardi Magni Epistolæ XIV*, Amsterdam, 1857, p. 117). The letter furnishes good evidence of the fact that astrology in the fourteenth century was much contaminated with magic (see pp. 118 ff.).

patristic hostility toward astrology culminated in the last quarter of the fifteenth century in the *Adversus Astrologos* of Pico della Mirandola. Spurred on by a religious conviction, this Platonic philosopher, himself an enthusiastic believer in the Jewish Cabala, attacked astrology with all the weapons which the centuries of warfare since the days of Cicero and Sextus Empiricus had invented.[1]

The polemic carried on against astrology by Petrarch and the theologians of the later centuries, restricting itself largely to religious and ethical arguments, failed to deal astrology a mortal blow. A distrust of the vulgar astrologer, it is true, came in time to be shared by every one. Literary satire in the later centuries found in the professional diviner a favorite victim—a fact for which Ariosto's *Il Nigromante,*[2] Rabelais' *Pantagruel,* and Swift's famous joke on the astrologer Partridge, stand witness. Benvenuto da Imola probably gives expression to the attitude of many in Petrarch's own century, when he says: 'Certe fateor quod astra non mentiuntur, sed astrologi bene mentiuntur de astris.'[3] At a time when astrological predictions were freely bought and sold, and when princes could bribe astrologers to write damaging horoscopes of their enemies,[4] many an employer must have suspected the honesty, if not the art, of his own hireling. But this scepticism of the practitioner did not impair the universal faith in astrology itself. Its theological opponents failed, in particular, to convince the scientist; and it was with the scientist that the final verdict rested. No astronomer of note, down to

[1] Pico della Mirandola is fully discussed in Soldati's *La Poesia Astrologica nel Quattrocento* (pp. 217-25).

[2] See especially a discussion of Act II, Scene 1, by Marpillero, in *Giorn. Stor.* 33. 307.

[3] Quoted by Burckhardt (2. 371).

[4] Several amusing illustrations of this are found in Gabotto's essay (*Riv. di Fil. Scient.* 8. 382 ff.).

the time of Kepler,[1] dared to question the reality of astrology. Most astronomers, in fact, carried on their studies as an adjunct to the more lucrative trade of reading horoscopes. John of Saxony, a Parisian astronomer of the fourteenth century, felt it necessary to defend the publication of a purely astronomical work by emphasizing its utility for the practical science of judgments.[2] In time, to be sure, astronomers made more and more of a distinction between general and particular predictions, and became sceptical about the latter.[3] Francis Bacon, in the sane astrology which he commends in his *De Augmentis Scientiarum*,[4] abolished prognostications of single events altogether. But science never refuted the fundamental principles of astrology. Men of letters, too, were often its enthusiastic supporters. Boccaccio, to whom Petrarch had addressed many of his diatribes, was a firm believer in stellar influence.[5] When, in 1410, Poggio brought to light the first manuscript of Manilius, humanists vied with one another in producing commentaries.[6] Poggio himself was

---

[1] Herz, *Kepler's Astrologie*, Vienna, 1895. Even Galileo wrote horoscopes at the Medicean court (Soldati, p. 117, note).

[2] Duhem 4. 84.

[3] Soldati, p. 116.

[4] Spedding and Robertson, *The Philosophical Works of Francis Bacon* (London, 1905), p. 464.

[5] Boccaccio's belief in astrology is discussed in some detail in Tatlock's *The Scene of the Franklin's Tale Visited* (pp. 24, 28); cf. A. Graf, *Miti, Leggende, e Superstizioni del Medio Evo* (Turin, 1893) 2. 169-95. Boccaccio espouses such astrological doctrines as that Venus produces acute intellects and liberal dispositions (*De Genealogiis Deorum*, It. tr., Venice, 1580, fol. 52b); that Mars causes wars and failures of crops (*ibid.*, fol. 146b; cf. fols. 14b, 53 ff.); that the ancient belief in gods arose from a deification of the planets (*Vita di Dante*, ed. Moutier, p. 52; cf. pp. 29, 81); and that only the existence of stellar influence can account for the infinite diversity of human talents (*Commento sopra Dante*, ed. Moutier 1. 71-2; cf. 2. 55-6).

[6] Soldati, p. 130 ff.

a convert to astrology.[1] So were Tasso[2] and Pontano. The
De Rebus Cœlestibus of Pontano, written in refutation of
Pico della Mirandola's attack, is judged by a recent critic[3]
to be a masterpiece of logical reasoning. It constitutes,
perhaps, the culmination of that philosophical defense of
Christian astrology which had been in the making since the
time when Albert the Great boldly accepted the new science
of the Moors.

But to trace the history of astrology through the fifteenth
and sixteenth centuries is not our task. During the Renaissance, astrology enjoyed once more that universal reign
which it had held in the Roman Empire. In the long warfare between theology and the science of the stars, the
latter had fairly conquered. The final disproof of astrology was never written. So long as the cosmology of
Aristotle, and the geocentric astronomy of Ptolemy, held
sway in mediæval schools, a refutation was impossible.
With the arrival of the new astronomy of Copernicus, it was
no longer necessary.

[1] *Epist.* 9. 16 (ed. Tonelli, 1859).
[2] Belloni, *Il Seicento* (Milan, no date), p. 8.
[3] Soldati, p. 253.

CHAPTER VI

ASTROLOGERS IN MEDIÆVAL ENGLAND

Italy, peculiarly exposed by reason of its geographical position, had early become infested with a host of astrologers and magicians, which she, in turn, transmitted to her northern neighbors, France and England. This process of migration was, however, a slow one. In the study of scientific astronomy, indeed, the universities of Paris and Oxford were in advance of those of Bologna and Padua.[1] But the sober scholars of the North, practising astrology as a part of the accepted astronomical science of the day, were still at a far remove from the professional necromancers in the employ of an Italian prince. It seems that not until the middle of the fourteenth century could the royal court of France boast an astrologer of the type of Guido Bonatti. And in England, which was separated by a further degree from contact with the Moorish East, astrology never acquired that position of prominence which it occupied in southern Europe. The vernacular literature of England before 1350 affords few references to it that do not go back to literary sources. Even after that date astrology probably remained a thing more talked about by the learned and the literary than seen in practice.

All the greater interest, therefore, attaches to those few indications which do exist of the presence in mediæval England of actual astrologers. At the University of Oxford, of course, the science was well known, although it did not occupy nearly so exalted a place in the curriculum as at the universities of Bologna and Padua.[2] Robert Grosse-

[1] Cf. Duhem 4. 182-5.

[2] The list of text-books on astrology at Oxford, given by Rashdall (*Universities of Europe*, Oxford, 1895, 2. 458), contains no

teste and Roger Bacon in the thirteenth century, and Bradwardine and Wyclif[1] in the fourteenth, were thoroughly
versed in matters astrological. Traveling scholars, furthermore, like Adelard, Robert de Retines, and Alexander
Neckam, must have fostered scientific studies. Of Adelard,
for example, we know that he made his home at Bath, and
that his treatise on the astrolabe was probably dedicated
to the English prince, Henry Plantagenet.[2]

We fortunately possess a concrete indication of the state
of astrological learning at the close of the twelfth century
in reports found in several English chronicles for the year
1186. All Europe, it appears, had been cast into a
panic by reason of a prediction, published broadcast by
the astrologers, of an approaching conjunction of planets
in the constellation Libra. The fact that the conjunction
was to take place in an 'airy' or 'windy' sign was interpreted as signifying, in addition to many other evils, a
terrific wind-storm. A German chronicler relates that
people for very fear built themselves caves underground,
and that special services were held in many churches.[3]
The English chroniclers, Roger of Hoveden[4] (1174-1201)
and Benedict of Peterborough,[5] repeat the prediction of an
astrologer Corumphira (his nationality is not indicated),
who prophesied an earthquake for some countries and a
terrific wind for others. Cities in sandy regions were to
be completely overwhelmed, and Egypt and Ethiopia were

specifically astrological works. The list for Bologna (Rashdall
1. 249), on the other hand, includes such well known texts as the
Isagoge of Alchabitius, Ptolemy's *Quadripartitum,* and the *Tractatus
Astrolabii* of Messahala, which is the treatise translated by Chaucer.

[1] See below, pp. 124 ff.
[2] Haskins, *Adelard of Bath and Henry Plantagenet* (*Eng. Hist.
Rev.* 28. 516).
[3] *Die Jahrbücher von Marbach* (ed. G. Grandaur, Leipzig, 1896),
p. 8.
[4] *Chronica* (ed. Stubbs, Rolls Ser.) 2. 290-2.
[5] *Gesta Regis Henrici Secundi* (ed. Stubbs, Rolls Ser.) 1. 324-5.

to become uninhabitable. 'Let each person be assured,' says Corumphira, 'that the conjunction about to take place, whatever others may say, signifies to me, if God so wills, the mutation of kingdoms, the superiority of the Franks, the destruction of the Saracenic race, with the superior blessedness of the religion of Christ, and its especial exaltation, together with longer life to those who shall be born hereafter.' In Hoveden's chronicle there is added another prognostication by an English astrologer, William, clerk to John, the constable of Chester. William is no more restrained than his fellow-prophet in predicting the direst happenings on all sides. His prognostication bristles with technical jargon.[1] 'Inasmuch as Mars is being scorched by the orb of the Sun,' William concludes his prophecy, 'being thus impeded and embarrassed between two evils, Saturn and the Tail of the Dragon, he becomes infected with their nature, and signifies sorrows, contentions, alarms, catastrophes, murders, and spoliation of property. The Tail also signifies separations, losses, dangers, and diminution of possessions. Because Mars forms an evil conjunction with the Tail in the ascendant, I do therefore contradict the judgment pronounced by Albumasar upon this figure in the *Centiloquium*[2]: "Turn your eyes from the figure in which Mars is at the greatest angle when Scorpio or the Tail is in the ascendant." And as it is evident to every astrologer that Saturn rules over this climate, the Moon participating with him, I am of opinion that this land cannot be considered exempt from the impending evil. Wherefore, the only remedy remaining is for princes to be on their guard, to serve God, and to flee the devil, that so the Lord may avert their imminent punishments.'

[1] *Chronica* 2. 292-3.

[2] The *Centiloquium*, of course, was not ascribed to Albumasar, but to Ptolemy. William is in general pretending to more learning than he possessed. The *Centiloquium*, as we have it, contains no aphorism similar to that quoted.

Hoveden asserts that terror was widespread at the approach of September, when the conjunction was expected to take place. Some comfort was gained from a more reassuring prediction made by a Saracen astrologer, Pharamella, which he sent to John, Bishop of Toledo. Pharamella takes his northern colleagues to task for blundering in their calculations. He accuses them, in particular, of leaving out of account the respective situations of Mars and Venus. Mars, he says, on the day of the conjunction, will not be in Libra, but in the thirteenth degree of Virgo; while Venus in Scorpio, which is the house of Mars, will entirely neutralize his evil influence.[1] The fact that Libra is a 'windy' sign, Pharamella asserts, means nothing. Gemini and Aquarius are also 'windy' signs, and yet the recent conjunctions in those constellations produced no harm. He advises the astrologers of the North to keep abreast of the times in the matter of astrological literature, and to read the tables of Hermes, Astales, and Albumasar. He calls upon them to stop their dreaming and to relinquish their false opinions, or else be converted to the religion of Ishmael. And he ends his letter with the words: 'According to the judgment of Messahala and Alkindi, unless God shall ordain it otherwise, there will be a scanty vintage, crops of wheat of moderate average, much slaughter by the sword, and many shipwrecks.'

Because of the positive tone employed by the Moorish astrologer, the editor of Hoveden[2] suspects that this letter may have been written after the dangerous day had passed. At any rate, very little out of the ordinary happened in the year 1186. The French chronicler Rigord says that the predictions of the astrologers were entirely discredited,[3] and the author of the *Annales Marbacenses* adds the com-

[1] *Chronica* 2. 297.
[2] *Chronica* 2. 299.
[3] *Vie de Philippe-Auguste* (in Guizot's *Coll. des Mém. Relatif à l'Hist. de France,* Paris, 1825, 12. 63).

ment: 'ut probaretur sapientia mundi hujus stultitiam esse apud Deum.'[1] Other writers found some justification for the astrologers' apprehensions in the victories of Saladin in the Holy Land in 1187.[2]

Whether the astrological learning which William, the clerk of Chester, was so eager to exhibit, represented a widespread interest in the science among the English of the time, it were hard to tell. Certain it is that other references to astrology in the chronicles are few. One short notice is to be found in the *Miracula S. Thomæ Cantuariensis,* written by a monk, William, toward the close of the twelfth century. William relates how an Italian and his son, who were afflicted with the falling sickness, and who ascribed their malady to the evil influence of the stars, came for cure to the saint's tomb.[3] William takes occasion to preach a short sermon against astrology, employing the well-known arguments of the Church Fathers. Many diseases, he admits, vary in intensity according to the moon, but this is no excuse for accusing the stars of evil. All things made by God are good. Let the lunatic rather accuse the spirits of evil, who observe the phases of the moon to enter their victims.[4] From the other historical records of the time, little indeed can be gleaned except notices of comets and falling stars. A comet was said to have heralded the arrival of William the Conqueror in 1066[5]; another the death of Pope Urban in 1254.[6] In the year 1394, an unusually unlucky comet

[1] Benedict of Peterborough, *op. cit.* 1. 324, note.

[2] *Itinerarium Peregrinorum et Gesta Regis Ricardi* (ed. Stubbs, Rolls Ser.) 1. 6.

[3] *Materials for the History of Archbishop Thomas Becket* (ed. Robertson, Rolls Ser.) 1. 165.

[4] The passage is an excellent indication that the patristic view of astrology was far from disappearing immediately after the introduction of the new astrology.

[5] *Eulogium Historiarum* (ed. Haydon, Rolls Ser.) 3. 45.

[6] *Ibid.* 1. 391.

appeared, which caused a drought, and was connected with a defeat of the Franks in Turkey.[1] Mention is also made of a conjunction of Jupiter and Saturn in the year 1385, which, as the chronicle maintains, was soon followed by a great 'commotion of realms.'[2]

For the second half of the fourteenth century, the dearth of information on the subject of astrologers in England finds some compensation in a corresponding wealth of historical notices for France. During the reign of King Charles V, the Italian court-astrologer, migrating from the South, had made himself at home in the households of French noblemen. King Charles V himself was a patron of astrology, and one of his prominent courtiers was an Italian astrologer, Thomas of Pisa, who received at the king's hands a monthly salary of a hundred francs.[3] The royal library of eleven thousand volumes contained many astrological texts, among others the *Quadripartitum* and *Centiloquium* of Ptolemy, and works by Guido Bonatti and Hali Abenragel.[4] The extravagances of astrological practice at the royal court even called forth the satire of a contemporary poet, Phillippe de Mézières. He advises the

---

[1] *Ibid.* 1. 286-7.

[2] *Chronicon Angliæ* 1328-88 (ed. Thompson, Rolls Ser.), p. 364.

[3] Tiraboschi, *Storia della Letteratura Italiana* (Venice, 1823-5) 5. 285. Christine of Pisa, the daughter of the Italian astrologer, wrote a famous biography of Charles V, in which she praises him for his patronage of the sciences, incidentally exhibiting her own unbounded enthusiasm for her father's particular art: 'Et, en ce, nous appert une prérogative d'astrologie vers les autres sciences; car les choses dont elle considere sont naturellement à tous merveillables, et naturellement tous hommes les désirent savoir; aussi, et que, par elles sceues, on cognoist grant partie de la naissance des choses de ça bas' (*Livre des Fais et Bonnes Meurs du Sage Roy Charles V* 1. 77: Petitot's *Coll. des Mém.*, Paris, 1825, 6. 128; cf. 5. 208; 6. 8).

[4] Lebeuf, *De L'Astrologie qui avait Cours sous Charles V* (Leber, *Coll. des Diss.* 15. 402 ff.); cf. Jorga, *Philippe de Mézières et la Croisade au XIVe Siècle* (Paris, 1896), p. 419.

king, specifically, to avoid an abominable superstitious belief of the English, who held, he says, that a man would have bad luck all the week if some one made a face at him on Monday.[1]   Nicolas Oresme, the great French economist and Bishop of Liseux, wrote a series of treatises against astrology, the purpose of which was to prevent Charles V from placing too much confidence in his Italian advisers.[2] But Nicolas Oresme, though he represents on the subject of astrology the conservative scientific opinion of his time, and though he was quite severe in denouncing magic and the extreme forms of judicial astrology, was himself compelled to accept astrology in theory.   Consequently his polemic can have had little effect.[3]

Simon de Phares, a chronicler of the late fifteenth century, has left us a list of the prominent astrologers living in France at the time of Charles V.[4]   This document, besides indicating the extent to which astrology was current at the French courts of Paris and Orleans,[5] contains a number of

[1] Lebeuf, *op. cit.*, p. 399.

[2] Ch. Jourdain, *Nicolas Oresme et les Astrologues de la Cour de Charles V* (*Rev. des Quest. Histor.* 10. 136-59).

[3] A summary of Oresme's vernacular treatise on divination is given by Meunier (*Essai sur La Vie et les Ouvrages de Nicole Oresme,* Paris, 1857, pp. 48 ff.).   It affords the best possible proof of the fact that even the most enlightened scientific minds of Europe in the Middle Ages were powerless to rid themselves of the belief in astrology.   Oresme can, of course, condemn predictions *per certitudinem,* and the system of *electiones,* when utilized for magic, by appealing to the current Church doctrine on the subject. But if the astrologers confine themselves to predicting the individual's 'inclinations' and 'complexions,' Oresme exempts them from censure.   Oresme's best argument, in general, is that the science of astrology is still too undeveloped to be worthy of much confidence.   Even in predicting the weather, mariners are more successful than astrologers.

[4] Published in part by Lebeuf, in his article, *De L'Astrologie qui avait Cours sous Charles V* (pp. 400-8).

[5] The notices found in Simon de Phares on astrology at Orleans may be of interest in connection with the clerk of Chaucer's

direct references to England, thus furnishing a valuable historical background for that sudden interest in astrology shown by the English writers of the latter half of the fourteenth century. The almost continuous wars between France and England find frequent mention in Simon's chronicle. Thus Maistre Michel de Jalongues is said to have predicted the inundations of the Rhone, 'et l'eslevation des Anglois et Bretons qui se misdrent sus pour expeller les barbares qui furent desconfis devant l'an 1374.'[1] Maistre Marc de Gennes, an astrologer of Paris, prophesied the outcome of the battle of Rosebecque, and also predicted the death of Edward the Black Prince.[2] The battle of

Franklin's Tale, who, it will be remembered, was a 'bachelor of lawe' at Orleans. The chronicle of Simon makes no mention of the university, but indicates that the house of Orleans was a patron of astrologers. Thus of Maistre Gilbert de Chasteaudun (Lebeuf, p. 401) it is said that he was 'moult aprecié en la maison d'Orléans pour la science des estoilles.' Again (p. 404), 'Messire Pierre de la Bruyere fut en ce temps à Orléans moult estimé des nobles et du clergié, fist en son temps plusieurs instrumens servant à la théorie.' Of still a third astrologer it is said that he retired to Orleans at the close of his life: 'Cestui de Saint-Mesmin fut bien souffisant astrologien, et composa de beaux traictiez; mais en les viels jours laissa la félicité mondaine et se rendit reclus à Orléans' (p. 405). It would be interesting to know whether Orleans, in addition to being a general haven for astrologers, also fostered the occult sciences at the university. The poet Deschamps was a 'clerk of Orleans,' and if the interpretation made by one of his editors (G. Raynaud, editor of the last four volumes of *Oeuvres Completes*, 1882; see II. 148) of *Balade 225* (*op. cit. 2.* 52) is correct, himself practised astrology in his youth. Hœpffner (*Eustache Deschamps: Leben und Werke*, Strassburg, 1904, p. 28) doubts whether any literal interpretation of the ballade is justified. These slight indications that Orleans was a centre of astrology may be added to those mentioned by Professor Tatlock in *The Scene of the Franklin's Tale Visited* (pp. 41-4).

[1] Lebeuf, p. 401.

[2] *Ibid.*, p. 403: 'Cestui aussi prédit la mort du noble Edoard, prince de Galles, qui puis fust roy d'Angleterre et d'Hybernie, qui trespassa l'an 1376.'

Cocherel (1363), between the English and Bertrand du Guesclin, was foreseen by Maistre Jacques de Saint-André.[1] Of two astrologers, it is said expressly that they visited England, one of them for the purpose of amusing King John, then a captive at London:

Maistre Pierre de Valois, résidant à Coucy, homme de singuliere estude et moult aprecié des Anglois, et depuis du roy Charles le Quint pour la science des estoilles. Cestui ala souvent en Angleterre pour plusieurs différants, et prédist plusieurs choses comme est assis par ses pronostications sur les révolutions de l'an 1360. Cestui sur la révolution de l'an 1358, pronostica de la Jacquerie, qui commença en Beauvoisin, par les communes sur les gentilshommes, le 28 jour de may, ou dit an, ce qui advint, car ils tuèrent tous les nobles et les femmes et les enfans.[2]

Maistre Guillaume de Loury, résident à Bourges, fut envoyé querir, pour son grant sçu et singulieres expériences de sa science des estoilles, par les Anglois, et y ala voulentiers, pour que cestoit pour desennuyer le bon roy Jehan, qui fut prins à Poitiers, le lundy 19 de septembre 1356, comme il avoit prédit. En son temps pronostica ou mois d'avril 1351, et derechief, encore une autre fois, l'an ensuivant fut encore resconfit li Anglois et Gascons. Il advertit aussi messire Charles d'Espaigne, connestable de France, qui ne le voulut croire, et fut tué en une hostellerie, en la ville de Laigle en Normandie, par les gens et du consentement du roy de Navarre; prédist aussi la desconfiture de Messire Robert de Clermont, lieutenant du duc de Normandie, et la mort de messire Geffroy de Harecourt.[3]

Apart from the slight notices given by Simon de Phares, the history of professional astrologers in mediæval England remains largely a matter of conjecture. It is indeed difficult to discover further traces of astrologers in the contemporary historical documents until the close of the fifteenth century. In the year 1503, a follower of Edmund de la Pole confessed at a trial that previous to following his master to the continent, he had consulted an astrologer regarding Edmund's probable future, but that he had

[1] *Ibid.*, p. 406.
[2] *Ibid.*, p. 405.
[3] *Ibid.*, p. 404.

obtained no satisfactory reply because he was ignorant of Edmund's hour of birth.[1]   At another trial, some years earlier, a certain Bernard Vignolles tells how the traitor Kendal, with two helpers, hired an astrologer in Italy to do away secretly with Henry VII and his family[2]—a plan that was cleverly frustrated by Bernard himself.   In the sixteenth century—as the stories go to prove which gather about the famous English astrologer, Dr. Dee—alchemists, magicians, and astrologers plied their trade as freely in England as in the rest of Europe.

[1] *Letters and Papers Illustrative of the Reigns of Richard III and Henry VII* (ed. Gairdner, Rolls Ser.) 1. 226 ff.

[2] *Ibid.* 2. 318.   The story is in itself amusing.   Bernard was sent by the Italian astrologer to England with a box of magic ointment. He found the stuff so foul-smelling that he threw it away and bought a substitute at Orleans.   Kendal, upon receipt of the box, went through a lot of hocus-pocus, all of which, of course, came to nothing.

CHAPTER VII

ASTROLOGY IN THE MEDIÆVAL ROMANCES

Long before the astrology of the Arabs found a home in the universities of Oxford and Paris, it had become the subject of song and story in the hands of the gleeman. The Crusades and the wars with the Moors of Spain had early brought the West into contact with the Orient, and stories of the learned magic of the East must have been current among the people many decades before Adelard of Bath and Herman of Dalmatia returned with the first Arabian text-books. Already in the *Chanson de Roland,* the Saracens are credited with the practice of diabolic arts: Archbishop Turpin, in the battle of Roncesvalles, kills the enchanter Siglorel, 'who once had been in hell, whither Jupiter had led him.'[1] In the Spanish epic, *Fernan Gonçalez,* the Moors are represented as astrologers in league with the devil.[2] The romances of the twelfth and thirteenth centuries habitually connect astrology and necromancy with the Moorish East. Chrétien's *Cligés,* in describing Fenice's skilful nurse, Thessala, names Thessaly as the home of necromancy, and the land where the devil's arts are taught, and where charms are made.[3] In the *Floovent,* a story of the wars between Christians and

---

[1] *Chanson de Roland* 1390-3 (ed. Gautier, Paris, 1884, p. 126):

> 'Et l'arcevesque lur ocist Siglorel,
> L'encanteür ki ja fut en enfer;
> Par artimal l'i cunduist Jupiter.'

[2] *Fernan Gonçalez* 473 ff. (Marden, *Palma de Fernan Gonçalez,* Baltimore, 1904, p. 69; cf. Comfort, *The Saracens in Christian Poetry: Dublin Rev.* 149. 27).

[3] *Cligés* 3002-10 (ed. Förster, Halle, 1884, pp. 120-1); cf. Easter, *A Study of the Magic Elements in the Romans d'Aventure and the Romans Bretons* (Baltimore, 1906), p. 17.

Moors, an old pagan doctor, Jacob, possesses the power of prophecy by reason of his astrological knowledge.[1] The Saracen maidens, furthermore, who appear so frequently in the *chansons de geste*, rescuing the captive Christians, are usually well versed in the magic sciences; and since they employ their talents in the service of true believers, are rarely censured for their diabolic lore. Flordespine, the daughter of the Saracen king, Machabre, although only fourteen years old, knows how to speak Latin and 'Romance,' to play at chess, and to read the courses of the stars and shining moon.[2] Galienne, the betrothed of the Christian Mainet, is similarly endowed with learning; it is by foreseeing the future in the stars that she is able to save her lover from a treacherous assault.[3] In the *Ipomedon*—a French romance of the last quarter of the twelfth century, translated several times into English—a king Adrastus comes to a tournament from Greece, and brings with him his Eastern astrologer, Amphiaraus, who unfortunately, however, gets his 'terms' confused, and fails to foresee his master's defeat.[4]

[1] *Floovent* 739 ff. (ed. Guessard et Michelant, 1859, p. 23). *Floovent* dates from the twelfth century.

[2] *Gaufrey* 1793 ff. (ed. Guessard et Chabaille, 1859, p. 55). *Gaufrey* is assigned to the thirteenth century.

[3] *Mainet* (*Romania* 4. 305 ff.; cf. 329, 333). *Mainet* dates from the early twelfth century. In the English Charlemagne-romances the Saracen maiden, Floripas, feeds the captive Christians with the aid of her magic girdle; cf. Caxton's *Charles the Grete* (*EETS. ES.* 36. 123); *The Sowdone of Babylone* (*EETS. ES.* 38. 68).

[4] *Ipomedon* 5574-90 (ed. Kölbing und Koschwitz, Breslau, 1889, p. 94). The earliest of the three English versions (all edited by Kölbing, Breslau, 1889), *Ipomadon*, written about 1350 (Wells, p. 146), alters the names to Aryns and Anferas (4197, 4203). In the OF. romance, *Partonopeus de Blois* (dated about 1188), Egypt is referred to (7220: ed. Crapelet 2. 75) as a home of astronomy and magic (the reference is not found in the ME. version, written about 1450). The late OF. romance, *Cleomades*, introduces three Eastern kings, who are versed in astronomy and necromancy (ed. Hasselt, Brussels, 1895, pp. 52, 58).

One of the early tales of the *Roman de Renart* (Branch X, dating from the early thirteenth century) is particularly interesting in that it alludes to the position held by astrology in the medical schools of contemporary Italy. The Fox, wishing to regain favor with King Noble, appears at court in the rôle of physician, promising the sick monarch a sure recovery. He wins the confidence of his client by the pretense that he has just returned from a period of study at the university of Salerno, and that he knows astronomy.[1] In a later continuation of the *Roman* (Branch XXIII, dated about 1300), Renart actually does venture abroad in search of learning, and becomes an adept in necromancy at the famous school of magic at Toledo by secretly watching a pagan conjurer at his work in a hidden cell.[2]

Even more directly traceable to an Eastern source are the astrological references in certain collections of Oriental tales. The legend of *Barlaam and Josaphat,* popularized for the West by the *Legenda Aurea* of Jacobus à Voragine (1230-98), and found in three Middle English versions, leads us back to a Greek text, written probably in Syria in the eighth century.[3] When in the course of the story—itself based upon a long Oriental tradition—it is related how an astrologer prophesied the future of the young prince, Josaphat, an evident attempt is made by the author of the Greek version to reconcile the incident with the beliefs of the Christian Church. 'Thus spake the astrol-

[1] *Roman de Renart* 10. 1524 ff. (ed. Martin, Strassburg, 1882, I. 384).

[2] *Roman de Renart* 23. 1172 ff. (ed. Martin 2. 311).

[3] The most recent summary of the investigations on the subject of this legend (in the edition of John of Damascus by Woodward and Mattingly, Loeb Class. Ser., London, 1914) ascribes the original *Barlaam and Josaphat* (p. XII) with some confidence to John of Damascus (died 754), among whose works it has often been printed. On the ME. versions, see Wells, p. 806.

oger,' he says, 'like Balaam of old, not that his star-lore told him true, but because God signifieth the truth by the mouth of his enemies.'[1] All the many retellings of the story preserve this pious comment.[2] An exact parallel to it, in fact, is found in the *Dolopathos,* one of the several extant versions of the collection of Eastern tales usually known by the name of the *Seven Sages.* Here the astrologer who foretells the future greatness of the emperor's son, Lucimien, is also compared to Balaam, and his prophetic powers are said to be a direct gift from God, and not a result of his science.[3] The author of the *Dolopathos,* however, soon forgets to insert orthodox caveats, and the *Dolopathos,* as well as the several versions of the *Seven Sages* in French and English, is full of references to magic and astrology.[4]

The romances of Alexander constitute another cycle of tales that trace their origin to the East. All of the Western versions go back to a Greek account, the *Pseudo-Callisthenes,* written probably in the third century of our era—a time when astrology was still current in the

[1] *Barlaam and Joasaph* (ed. Woodward and Mattingly), p. 7.

[2] The three ME. versions are printed in Horstmann's *Altenglische Legenden* (Paderborn, 1895).

[3] Johannis de Alta Silva, *Dolopathos* (ed. Oesterley, Strassburg, 1873), p. 12; cf. the OF. version 1151 ff. (ed. Brunet, Paris, 1856, p. 41). The author of the Latin version lived about 1207-12; the author of the French, about 1220-6. The *Dolopathos* is not represented in English.

[4] It is by looking 'unto the sternes and to þe mone' that the wise masters, in one of the English versions, discover the wicked empress' design against their pupil, Florentine. The latter in a similar fashion learns that if he can remain mute seven days he will be saved (*Seven Sages of Rome* 400 ff.: ed. Campbell, 1907, p. 14; cf. pp. 74, 89). Cf. also the version edited by Wright (Percy Soc., 1845), pp. 11, 12, 64. The French version as a whole contains more astrology than the imitations in ME. (cf. Brunet, pp. 55, 66).

Byzantine empire. Even in this, its earliest extant form, the story had embodied the legend of Alexander's descent from the Egyptian sorcerer, Nectanabus. Throughout the early portion of the narrative, in which is related the arrival of Nectanabus at the Macedonian court, and the deceits by means of which he became the father of the future king, astrology plays an important part. Succeeding redactors of the legend dealt variously with these astrological details. The Christian writers, one and all, took delight in the closing episode of the story of Nectanabus, in which the sorcerer, after having prophesied by the stars that he would be killed by his own son, is thrown into a ditch by Alexander, and taunted for his impious beliefs.[1] In the more technical details of the story, imitators of the *Pseudo-Callisthenes* were not always successful. One curious misunderstanding of the astrological terms of the Greek is already to be found in the Latin life of Alexander, written by Archpresbyter Leo in the tenth century, and known by the name of *Historia de Prœliis*. The *Pseudo-Callisthenes*, namely, in describing an astrolabe of Nectanabus, and picturing its various discs, had spoken of one circle as representing the astrological 'decans' (δεκανούς).[2] The Christian translator, in his ignorance, understood the Greek to be δέκα νοῦς, and translated it with 'decem intelligentias.' Some of Leo's followers, notably the author of the *Wars of Alexander,* repeated this curious mistake.[3] The French versions of the legend are more

---

[1] A taunt which in reality, of course, merely added to the dramatic irony of the scene. The three English versions relate this portion of the tale; cf. *Wars of Alexander* 708 ff. (*EETS. ES.* 47. 24); *Alisaunder* 1072 ff. (*EETS. ES.* i. 212); *Kyng Alisaunder* 710 ff. (Weber, *Metrical Romances,* Edinburgh, 1810, i. 34); cf. Wells, p. 98 ff.

[2] Divisions of the signs into ten equal parts.

[3] *The Wars of Alexander* speaks of 'twelve undirstandings' (274: ed. Skeat, *EETS. ES.* 47. 9). Skeat defines the word simply as 'an astrological term.'

enlightened on matters astrological; the author of the English *Kyng Alisaunder,* imitating the French *Roman de Toute Chevalerie,* is able to refer to the mysterious instrument of Nectanabus as an 'ars-table.'[1] When Gower, finally, retells the story of Nectanabus in the *Confessio Amantis,*[2] the astrological possibilities of the story are fully exploited. He describes the astrolabe of the sorcerer with scientific detail, and airs his learning as he pictures the magician's conjurings.

The astrology and magic of the East, finding their way into the popular literature of France and England by various channels, soon made themselves at home in the whole realm of mediæval romance. They easily established friendly relations with the Celtic magic of the *matière de Bretagne,* and it was not long before the fairies and dwarfs of Northern folk-lore were as learned as the daughters of the Saracens.[3] The precise point of time when the magic of the East became mingled with the indigenous magic of the West is, of course, difficult to determine. A work so

[1] *Kyng Alisaunder* 287 (Weber, *Metrical Romances* I. 17). The *Kyng Alisaunder* was written before 1330, and 'ars-table' is probably the first appearance of the word 'astrolabe' in English. The earliest citation in the *NED.* is under the year 1366.

[2] *Conf. Am.* 6. 1790 ff. (ed. Macaulay, Oxford, 1901, 3. 215 ff.).

[3] Several instances of fairies who are expert in the sciences of magic and astrology will appear in the following pages. A few more may be added here. The 'fairy of the white hands' in *Le Bel Inconnu* has been instructed by her father in the seven arts, and especially in necromancy and astrology (1918, 4846: ed. Hippeau, 1860, pp. 68, 172). In the shorter English imitation, *Libeaus Desconus,* although sorcery plays a part (cf. 1513, 1780, 1795: ed. Kaluza, Leipzig, 1890, pp. 84, 99, 100; cf. Wells, pp. 71, 772), astrology is not specifically mentioned. Melior, the fairy in the English *Partonope of Blois* (about 1450; the French source is dated about 1188), learned the marvelous arts of the East from her father, the Emperor of Constantinople (5933: *EETS. ES.* 109. 225). Cf. also *Chanson d'Antioche* (ed. P. Paris, 1848), p. 59; and *Dolopathos* 9275.

purely Celtic as the *Mabinogion* is still free from astrology. So also are the *lais* of Marie de France, and, for the most part, the Arthurian romances of Chrétien de Troyes. A reference to astrology is found in the *Erec,* but Chrétien is careful to state that he is borrowing from Macrobius. Toward the close of the poem, Erec appears in a robe made by four fairies, who had portrayed thereon geometry, arithmetic, music, and astronomy. The last of these is called the chief of all the arts, and is described in words that remind us of the similar panegyric of Adelard of Bath:

> La quarte, qui aprés ovra,
> A mout buene œvre recovra;
> Car la mellor des arz i mist.
> D'astronomie s'antremist
> Cele qui fet tante mervoille,
> Qui as estoiles se consoille
> Et a la lune et au soloil.
> An autre leu ne prant consoil
> De rien qui a feire li soit;
> Cil la consoillent bien a droit.
> De quanque ele les requiert,
> Et quanque fu et quanque iert,
> Li font certainnement savoir
> Sanz mantir et sanz decevoir.[1]

In the romances dealing with the Tristan story, astrology is already an integral part of the *matière de Bretagne.* The dwarf Frocin, who appears in the French version of Béroul (1190-1200), is an expert astrologer.[2] When his plans for enticing Tristan and Iseult to betray themselves before the king have gone wrong, he is able to foresee his threatened disgrace in the stars. The *Tristan* of Thomas, on the other hand, though it also takes note of the tradition that the dwarf was an astrologer, is sceptical about his

---

[1] *Erec* 6777-6790 (ed. Foerster, Halle, 1896, p. 175); cf. above, p. 50.

[2] Béroul, *Roman de Tristan* 320 ff. (ed. Muret, Paris, 1913, p. 11).

having played the rôle of deceiver by the help of any such easy means.[1]

The process by which the astrology of the Orient became mingled with the simple magic of the Celts can be seen actually at work by comparing with one another the successive retellings of the Merlin legend. Although there are some traces of astrology in Geoffrey of Monmouth, the story of Vortiger's tower, and of the discomfiture of the magicians at the hands of the child Merlin, is still quite free from it. In the chronicles of Wace and Layamon, too, the *magi* of the Celtic tradition are simply 'wise men' and 'diviners.' When the legend, however, after having traveled to France, reappears in England in such works as the *Arthour and Merlin* (about 1325), and the prose romance of the fifteenth century, the *magi* of Geoffrey have turned definitely into astrologers. The *Arthour and Merlin*, differing somewhat from other versions of the story, makes a further curious use of astrology in the scene where Merlin confronts the wise men with the charge that they had sought to take his life. He exonerates them on the

---

[1] Bédier, *Le Roman de Tristan par Thomas* (Paris, 1902) 1. 192. Bédier paraphrases Gottfried von Strasburg's version (14, 244 ff.) as follows: 'Ce nain savoit, dit-on, lire, dans les étoiles les choses cachées, mais je ne veux rien rapporter de lui que ce que je trouve dans la vraie histoire: qu'il était adroit, rusé et bien emparlé.' On the question of dwarfs in mediæval romances, see A. Lütjens, *Der Zwerg in den Heldendichtungen des Mittelalters* (Breslau, 1911), p. 6; and Wohlgemuth, *Riesen und Zwerge in den Altfranzösischen Dichtungen* (Stuttgart, 1906), p. 80 ff. Schoepperle (*Tristan and Isolt: A Study of the Sources of the Romance*, London, 1913, 1. 249) thinks that the description of the dwarf in the *Tristan*, though, perhaps, reminiscent of the dwarfs in Celtic tradition, is based largely upon the contemporary custom of maintaining dwarfs at court. An interesting reference to astrology occurs in the *Tristan*, where the hero tells Iseult that his parents do not know of his whereabouts, since he had originally expected to go to Spain to study astronomy and other sciences (Bédier 1. 98).

ground that the sky itself was to blame for misleading them in their predictions:

> þe sky, þat ʒou schewed þat,
> It was þe fader, þat me biʒat;
> For he me hadde nouʒt to his wille,
> þurch ʒou he wald do me spille[1];

Astrology is also mentioned in the romances of Merlin in connection with the fay Morgain. Like the Mohammedan enchantresses of the *chansons de geste,* she is versed in astronomy and necromancy.[2]

The attitude of the romances toward astrology hardly admits of logical analysis. A narrator was as little hampered in the Middle Ages by questions of science or of ethics as he is to-day. It may be said, in general, that astrology, to the popular mediæval mind, was a wonderful science, vaguely defined, and seldom condemned, whose omnipotence was proverbial. It is spoken of everywhere as the chief of the seven arts, and was hardly distinguished from necromancy and magic. The reality of its powers was never doubted. By reason of its being a learned foreign importation, as yet somewhat removed from the life of the uneducated, and not subjected to the satire which it inevitably encountered in practice, astrology could acquire a fame in popular literature even exceeding that which it held among the astronomers of the schools. The common people who had not outgrown their faith in the simple magic of the Teutons and Celts—witness the serious defense of the belief in fairies, made by the author of the *Melusine*[3]—were not likely to be sceptical of the scientific

[1] *Arthour and Merlin* 1583-6 (ed. Kölbing, Leipzig, 1890, p. 47); cf. *Prose Merlin* (ed. Wheatley, *EETS.* 10. 39).

[2] *Prose Merlin* (*EETS.* 21. 375); cf. Paton, *Studies in the Fairy Mythology of Arthurian Romance* (*Radcliffe Coll. Monographs,* 1903), p. 46, note. The witch Carmile, appearing in the *Arthour and Merlin* (Kölbing, p. 126), is an adept in necromancy.

[3] *Melusine,* chap. 1 (ed. Donald, *EETS. ES.* 68. 2). The author is Jean d'Arras, writing about 1382-94. In the English translation,

magic, newly arrived from the Orient. A serious work like the prose *Lapidaire* of Philippe de Valois could assert that only fools doubted the existence of magic powers in stones, herbs, and spoken words.[1] And the author of the famous *Image du Monde,*[2] which retained its popularity down to the time when Caxton translated it into English, undertakes to defend both magic and astrology from the attacks of the incredulous, as well as from those who ascribe all such wondrous things to the devil. He introduces the subject in connection with a description of Virgil as a magician[3]:

Virgyle dyde and made many grete mervaylles, whiche the herers shold holde for lesynges yf they herde them recounted; ffor they wolde not byleve that another coude doo suche thynge as theye coude not medle wyth. And whan they here speke of suche maters or of other that they see at their eyen and that they can not understonde ne knowe not thereof, anon they saye that it is by thelpe of the fende that werketh in suche maner, as they that gladly myssaye of peple of recommendacion. And also saye it is good not to conne suche thynges. But yf they knewe the science and manere, they wold holde it for a moche noble and right werke of nature, and without ony other espece of evyll. And whan they know not ne understonde the thinge, they say moche more evyl than well.

Certaynly who that knewe well astronomye, ther is nothyng in the world of which he coude enquyre by reson but he shold have

made a century later, we read: 'And he is not wyse that suche thinges supposeth to comprehende in his wit, and weneth that the mervaylles that ben thrugh the universal world, may nat be true, as it is said of the thinges that men calle ffayrees, and as it is of many other thinges, whereof we may not have the knowleche of alle them.'

[1] 'Et nus sages homs ne doit douter que Diex n'ait mis vertuz en pierres et en herbes et en paroles, et qui ce ne croit et il desdit, il fait que pechierres' (Pannier, *Les Lapidaires Français du Moyen Age,* Paris, 1882, p. 292).

[2] The work is dated 1266. There is a dispute as to whether the author's name is Gautier of Metz or Gossouin of Metz; cf. Prior's edition of Caxton's translation (*Mirrour of the World,* ed. Prior, *EETS. ES.* 110, pp. ix-x).

[3] Caxton's *Mirrour of the World* 3. 13 (ed. Prior, p. 160).

knowleche therof. And many thynges shold he doo that sholde seme myracles to the peple whiche that knewe nothynge of the science. I saye not but ther myght be wel don evyll by hym that coude it; ffor ther is none so good science but that myght be entended therin somme malyce,[1] and that he myght use it in evyll that wolde so applye hym therto. God made never so good a gospel but somme myghte torne it contrarye to trouthe; and ther is no thynge so true but somme myght so glose that it shold be to his dampnacion, who that wolde payne hym to do evyll, how wel it is no maystrye to do yll.

As regards the ethical question involved in the employment of astrology and magic, the view just expressed by the author of the *Image du Monde* is also that of the mediæval romances. Condemnations of astrology are rare. Removed from ecclesiastical influence, and not called upon to solve questions of right and wrong, the writer of the tales did not censure magic practices except when a condemnation was demanded by the story itself—that is, when magic was used for manifestly evil purposes. The dwarf in Béroul's *Tristan* is not spared a denunciation[2]; and the wizard Maugis, in the *Foure Sonnes of Aymon*, though he is willing to come to the aid of his friend Renaud even after he has forsworn his art, realizes that he may be damned for this in the end.[3] But, despite the fact that magic is often felt to be on the defensive, it is never condemned outright. In the *Aiol,* a French romance of the

---

[1] The *Image du Monde* elsewhere (2. 24: *op. cit.,* p. 116) denounces necromancy—which it defines properly as a conjuring of evil spirits—in more vigorous terms: 'This is a scyence that, who that gevyth hym therto to do evyl, hit gyveth hym the deth; ffor yf he taketh no hede therof, he shal be dampned body and sowle.' But one may note that here, too, it is only when used for evil ends that black magic is condemned. The *Image du Monde* has many other references to astrology; cf. 1. 13 (*op. cit.*, p. 40); 2. 33 (p. 128); 3. 8 (p. 144).

[2] Béroul, *Tristan* 643 ff. (ed. Muret, p. 19).

[3] *The Foure Sonnes of Aymon,* chap. 24 (ed. Richardson, *EETS. ES.* 44. 503). Cf. Wace's *Roman de Rou* 7537.

twelfth century, even a pious hermit interprets a dream by means of the stars.[1] The Earl of Poitiers in the *Melusine*, who is endowed with the power of astrological prophecy, sings praises to God for bestowing upon man so marvelous a gift.[2] Fairies, as is well known, could be good Christians. The fay Melusine, in the romance just mentioned, assures her lover that she 'is of God' and that her belief is 'as a Catholique beleve oughte for to be.'[3] The hero in *Partonope of Blois,* defending his fairy love Melior before the bishop, testifies that she always speaks reverently of God.[4]

This general leniency shown by the romances toward magic was not altogether to the liking of the Church. There were not wanting, in the fourteenth century as in our own, those who saw in the reading of novels a snare of the devil. An interesting bit of proof of this is found in a treatise against astrology[5]—the *Trilogium Astrologiæ Theologizatæ*—written by Gerson, the famous chancellor of the University of Paris in the early fifteenth century. Gerson laments the universal prevalence in his time of superstitions regarding magic, and tries to define its cause. This he discovers to be a general corruption of the popular

[1] *Aiol* 390 ff. (ed. Normant et Raynaud, Paris, 1877, p. 12).

[2] *Melusine*, chap. 4 (ed. Donald, *EETS. ES.* 68. 22).

[3] *Melusine*, chap. 6 (*op. cit.,* p. 31); cf. *Romans of Partenay* 460 ff. (ed. Skeat, *EETS.* 22. 23).

[4] *Partonope of Blois* 5761 ff. (ed. Bödtker, *EETS. ES.* 109. 219). In Melior are united the Celtic fay and the Oriental sorceress. She herself confesses (5933) that she is the daughter of a Byzantine emperor, from whom she acquired her knowledge of astrology and necromancy.

[5] Like the similar works of Nicolas Oresme, the treatise was not really directed against astrology itself, but against magic. Gerson, much as he probably wished it, was unable to disprove scientific astrology, and consequently was powerless to do more than to warn against charlatans, and to plead for moderation in the use of the science. See Schwab, *Johannes Gerson* (Würzburg, 1858), pp. 714-7.

imagination, due in part to the tempting of the devil himself, partly to the persistence of pagan customs, and finally to the reading of romances. Gerson defines romances as 'books written in the French tongue, relating in poetic form the deeds of military heroes—stories which are fictitious for the most part, and which serve rather to satisfy a hunger for novelty and admiration, than to foster a knowledge of the truth.'[1]

[1] 'Ex lectione quorundam Romanciorum, i. e., librorum compositorum in Gallico quasi poeticorum de gestis militaribus, in quibus maxima pars fabulosa est, magis ad ingerendam quandam novitatem et admirationem quam veritatis cognitionem' (Schwab, p. 717). Is this the earliest definition of the novel?

CHAPTER VIII

ASTROLOGY IN MIDDLE ENGLISH LITERATURE

However valuable the naïve references to astrology in the French romances of the twelfth and thirteenth centuries may be for defining the popular mediæval attitude toward the magic of the East, they are of comparatively small service in determining the state of feeling in England itself. All the Middle English romances dealing with astrology were translations from the French or Latin, and very few even of these bear a date earlier than 1350. For direct evidence concerning the attitude toward astrology in England during the thirteenth and fourteenth centuries, one must turn to the more indigenous literary productions of the time, although these, too, afford only a scanty gleaning. It is safe to assume, of course, that the vulgar astrology of the almanac—whose importation into England dates back to the time of Ælfric[1]—was already widely current.[2] But all evidence points toward the conclusion that an interest in astrology proper did not become general in the vernacular literature of England before the age of Gower and Chaucer. Not until the fifteenth century, in effect, are references to astrology as frequent in English as they were in the literature of France one or two centuries previous.

[1] See above, pp. 44 ff.

[2] The best proof of this can be found in the portions of a popular calendar for the year 1349, published by A. Hahn (*Archiv* 106. 349-51). In the manuscript, which contains, among other things, the source for a portion of Rolle's *Pricke of Conscience*, is found a poem of some thirty-nine lines on the influence of planets, giving advice on undertaking any enterprise when this or that planet rules the day or the hour. The astrology of the poem is not much above the level of the Old English treatises which we met in the *Leechdoms* (see above, p. 44).

It may seem strange, in view of this generalization, that one of the most enlightened discussions of astrology in Middle English is found in a work dated as early as the latter half of the thirteenth century. It occurs in a fragment on popular science, part of the *Legend of Michael* in the *Southern Legendary Collection*.[1] The lines which bear particularly upon astrology are found near its beginning, and constitute a paraphrase of the current Church doctrine on the subject of stellar influence. After a general cosmological explanation of the universe and an enumeration of the seven planets, the poet continues:

> Thurf gret wit of clergie here [the planets] names were furst
>   ifounde.
> For ech of the sovene mai gret vertu an urthe do,
> Bothe of weder and frut, as here poer is therto;
> And also men that beoth ibore under here miȝte iwis
> Schulle habbe diverse miȝte, and lyf, after that here vertu is,
> Summe lechours, and summe glotouns, and summe other manere;
> Natheles a man of god inwit of alle thulke him mai skere:
> For planetes ne doth non other bote ȝeveth in manes wille,
> To beo lither other god as here vertu wole to tille,
> And ȝyveth also qualité to do so other so,
> And noȝt for then by his inwit ech man may do.
> For such qualité hath noman to beo lechour other schrewe,
> That ne mai him witie ther aȝen, ac natheles so doth fewe.[2]

No source for any portion of this *Fragment on Popular*

---

[1] The passage is at times referred to by its opening line as 'The riȝte putte of helle.' The earliest manuscript dates about 1280-90 (cf. Wells, p. 294). The piece has been published several times: in Wright's *Popular Treatises on Science* (London, 1841, pp. 132-40); in a reprint of the earliest manuscript (*Laud* 108: *EETS.* 87. 311-22); in *Jahrb. für Rom. und Engl. Lit.* (13. 150); and in Mätzner's *Altenglische Sprachproben* (1. 136 ff.); cf. further, Wells, p. 835.

[2] Mätzner's *Altenglische Sprachproben* (Berlin, 1867) 1. 138. The poem continues with a description of the astrological characteristics of the days of the week. Tuesday and Saturday are pronounced bad for beginning things.

Science has yet been pointed out.[1] The fragment, as a whole, shows evident affinities with the French *Image du Monde,* probably written (1266) shortly before the *Legend of Michael* itself, and with the scientific works of Alexander Neckam (dated about 1200), upon which the *Image* is partly founded.[2] Neckam's discussion of astrological fatalism and free will, or the corresponding passages of the *Image,* may, indeed, have suggested the somewhat more elaborated statement of the English poet.[3] Only in the

---

[1] In Mätzner's *Altenglische Sprachproben* (1. 137), a slight connection is found to exist between it and Bede's *De Natura Rerum.*

[2] Several of the parallels between the *Legend* and the two foreign works may here be enumerated: 1. The statement of the *Legend of Michael* (483, EETS. 87. 313) that the sun is 165 times as large as the earth, is found in the *Image* (3. 18: Caxton, p. 170), and in Neckam's *De Naturis Rerum* (1. 8: Wright, p. 44), where, however, the number is 166. 2. When the English reads (397):

> for the leste sterre i wis
> In hevene, as the boc ous saith, more than the urthe is,

the *Image* (3. 19: p. 171) could again serve as model. 'There is none,' says the latter, 'so lytil of them [the stars] that ye may see on the firmament but that is gretter than all therthe is.' 3. The English (530 ff.), in explaining the nature of thunder, employs the illustration of a hot piece of iron giving off a hissing sound when thrust into water. This goes back eventually to Neckam's *De Laudibus Divinæ Sapientiæ* (3. 107 ff.), which, in turn, is copied by the *Image* (2. 28: p. 121). 4. The Middle English poem (493 ff.) visualizes the distance between the earth and heaven by saying that if Adam had started to make a journey to the sky, traveling forty miles a day, he would to-day still be 'a thousand mile and mo' from his goal. The same illustration is found in the *Image* (3. 19: p. 172) although the mathematical figuring is more exact (Adam walks twenty-five French miles, or fifty English miles, a day, and the distance by which he falls short is measured as 713 years).

[3] The corresponding passage of Neckam's *De Naturis Rerum* has been cited in an earlier chapter (p. 62); cf. especially the following: 'Sciendum etiam est quod, licet superiora corpora effectus quosdam compleant in inferioribus, liberum tamen arbitrium animæ non impellunt in ullam necessitatem hoc vel illud exequendi.' Cf. also *Image* 2. 32 (p. 126); 2. 33 (p. 129); and especially 3. 13

closing line, with its comment that few men make use of their will-power in their struggle against evil, is there a hint that the author was acquainted with the more recent views on the subject of astrology, found in such works as the *Summa Theologiæ* of Thomas Aquinas.[1] But whatever be the final verdict as to its source, the passage must be considered one of the earliest expressions in a European vernacular of the scholastic doctrine concerning astrological fatalism. In English, the subject is not again so fully discussed until the time of Barbour's *Bruce* and Gower's *Confessio Amantis;* and the somewhat similar popularization of the orthodox teaching regarding astrology and free will, found in Jean de Meun's *Roman de la Rose,* can at best have antedated the *Legend of Michael* by only a few years.[2]

While the reference to astrology in the *Legend of Michael* represents the contemporaneous teachings of the learned, other discussions of the subject in Middle English literature drew upon less modern sources. It is a common saying that the learned science of one century becomes the popular science of the next. The more popular the science, in fact, the farther behind the times will it be. Side by side with the most advanced views regarding astrology, there still existed the ecclesiastical conservatism of the early mediæval centuries. The passages in Middle English literature, dealing with astrology, present accordingly a considerable variety of opinions—a variety which finds its explanation only in the light of the whole history of mediæval astrology.

(p. 161) : 'Every man hath the power to drawe hym self to do well or to do evyll, whiche that he wylle, as he that hath fre liberte of that one and of that other.'

[1] Cf. *Summa* I. 115. 4: 'Pauci autem sunt sapientes, qui huius modi passionibus resistant. Et ideo astrologi, ut in pluribus vera possunt prædicere, et maxime in communi. Non autem in speciali: quia nihil prohibet aliquem hominem per liberum arbitrium passionibus resistere.'

[2] On the *Roman de la Rose,* see below, pp. 138 ff.

It is important, therefore, in turning to the vernacular discussions themselves, to keep the early history of mediæval astrology clearly in mind. As we have seen, this was divided chronologically into two distinct periods. In the first, extending to the middle of the twelfth century, astrology was known only as a diabolic art, which had been condemned by the Fathers of the early Church. Even when it was treated as a formidable philosophical theory by John of Salisbury and Abelard, it was denounced as a manifestation of pagan impiety. The arrival of Aristotle and of Arabian science changed all this. Astrology was accepted by the scientists of the Church in theory, and virtually in practice. The champions of astrology, however, were not bold enough to confront the traditional teaching of the Church with one diametrically opposed. Hence, instead of attempting a substitution of doctrines, they contented themselves with a superposition. The early Church had made no distinction between a true and a false astrology. The Church of the thirteenth century, by making just this distinction, was enabled to entertain an enthusiasm for the moderate science of Ptolemy, and to preserve, at the same time, pious scorn for astrological magic, and that manifestation of judicial astrology which it loosely defined as prediction *per certitudinem*. The vagueness inherent in this definition of orthodox astrology gave rise, in the later centuries, as we have noted, to plentiful confusions. Enthusiasts for the science, like Roger Bacon and Pierre d'Ailly,[1] could make their appeal under cover

---

[1] Pierre d'Ailly (1350-1420) is an excellent example of an important Churchman—d'Ailly presided at the Council of Constance (1415)— who was a firm believer in astrology. He even subscribed to Albumasar's horoscopes of the various religions, which we met in the writings of Roger Bacon. Pierre d'Ailly, to be sure, made an exception in the case of Christianity, which, he said, was not ruled over by the stars (Guignebert, *De Imagine Mundi Ceterisque Petri de Alliaco Geographicis Opusculis,* Paris, 1902, pp. 16-21).

of the same orthodoxy that served Petrarch, Oresme, and Pico della Mirandola as an excuse for their attacks.

Now, in the discussions of astrology in vernacular literature, this situation was still further complicated. The debate concerning astrology carried on by the learned could at least boast of a continuous development. After Thomas Aquinas had embodied the Arabian cosmology in his system, no ecclesiastical writer—unless, like Petrarch, he deliberately ignored these newer advances—dared again to launch against astrology an indiscriminate polemic. But the popular writings of the thirteenth and fourteenth centuries were under no obligation to keep abreast of contemporaneous scientific literature.[1] Isidore and John of Salisbury did not cease to be read on the subject of astrology, even though their conclusions had been superseded by those of Albert the Great and Thomas Aquinas.

An example of the persistence in the fourteenth century of the hostility toward astrology characteristic of the early Middle Ages, is found in the writings of Rolle of Hampole. Himself an educated man, and at one time a student at Oxford, he was in all probability acquainted with the astrological science of the day. A passage of the *Pricke of Conscience* even subscribes, vaguely though it be, to the current cosmology of the scholastic scientists.[2] Neverthe-

---

[1] A good illustration of this is the popular encyclopædia, the *Image du Monde*. Although it was contemporary with such Latin encyclopædias as those of Vincent of Beauvais and Bartholomæus Anglicus, it adopted as its principal source the *Imago Mundi* of Honorius Inclusus, written more than a century and a half previous (see above, pp. 61, 109).

[2] *Pricke of Conscience* 7596-7617 (ed. Morris, Berlin, 1863, p. 205). Rolle cites Bartholomæus Anglicus as the source for a passage on the starry and crystalline heavens. For the following lines, in which he declares that the movement of the heavens is necessary for life on earth, he names no authority, but it may well be that for this again the original is the *De Proprietatibus Rerum* (cf. *Batman uppon Bartholome,* fols. 121ª ff.). Nassyngton (*Religious*

less, when Rolle, in a treatise on the decalogue, deals with astrology proper, he condemns it outright, and classes it, as did the ecclesiastical writers from Isidore to Gratian, with witchcraft and divination. The occult arts are accused of transgressing the first commandment. 'Alswa in þis comandement,' says Rolle, 'es forbodyn to gyffe trouthe till sorcerye or till dyvynynges by sternys or by dremys, or by any swylke thynges. Astronomyenes byhaldes þe daye and þe houre and þe poynte þat man es borne in, and undir whylke syngne he es borne, and þe poynte þat he begynnes to be in, and by þire syngnes and oþer þay say þat that sall befall þe man afterwarde, bot theyre errowre es reproffede of haly doctours.' The expository tone employed by the author would lead one to suspect that it was directed to a public still as ignorant of astrology as that which had listened to Ælfric's explanation of the astrological problems of twins.[1]

Poem 43-4: *EETS*. 26. 61) takes the scholastic cosmology similarly for granted:

> The firmament þou made movande,
> To noresche all thyng þareundire lyfande.

[1] *EETS*. 20. 9; cf. above, pp. 11, 20, 46. An application of the first commandment to divination and sorcery is common in Middle English. It is found, for example, in the *Lay-Folks' Catechism* of Archbishop Thoresby (1357), as well as in the Wycliffite adaptation of this (*EETS*. 118. 34-5). The Latin of the Lambeth Canons, upon which these catechisms were founded, is the earliest text which I have yet discovered in which the first commandment is thus interpreted. The Lambeth canons date about 1281. 'In primo prohibetur omnis idolatria, cum dicitur, *Non habebis Deos alienos coram Me:* in quo prohibetur implicite omnia sortilegia et omnes incantationes cum superstitionibus characterum, et hujusmodi figmentorum' (*EETS*. 118. 33-5). Cf. also Myrc's *Instructions to Parish Priests* (*EETS*. 31. 27). In Robert of Brunne's *Handlyng Synne* (571 ff.: *EETS*. 119. 21), an application of the first commandment is made to the popular belief that three fairies foretell the child's future at birth. For the 'lewed men' to whom Robert of Brunne addressed his writing, this simple superstition probably

The fear of transgressing the bounds of strict orthodoxy was also the probable cause of an argument against astrological fatalism which Trevisa inserted into his translation of Higden's *Polychronicon*. In the third book of his chronicle, Higden introduces the legend of Alexander the Great, and repeats the story of the Egyptian astrologer Nectanabus. The close of the episode, together with Trevisa's orthodox comment, runs as follows[1]:

In a day whan Phelip was absent, Alisaundre prayed Nectanabus þat he wolde teche hym his craft, and he grauntede; and whan þey come in fere unto a deep water pitte, Alisaundre þrew the wicche in þe same pitte; and whan he was in þat pitte and deed woundede, he axede of Alisaundre why he dede so. 'Thy craft,' quod Alisaundre, 'is to blame, for he warnede þe not what schulde byfalle: þere þou liest nevelynge, and schuldest telle after þese þynges of hevene.' The whiche answerede and seide, 'No man may flee his own destayne. I knowe wel by þis craft þat myn owne sone schulde slee me.' *Trevisa.* Nectanabus seide þis sawe, and was a wicche, and þerfore it is nevere þe bettre to trowynge: but it were a vile schame for a Cristen man to trowe þis false sawe of þis wicche; for from every myshap þat man is ischape in þis worlde to falle ynne, God may hym save ʒif it is his wille.

We have seen, in our general survey of mediæval astrology, that the persistence of the early ecclesiastical fear of the practical science was frequently coupled with a generous acceptance of astrological theory. Such a juxtaposition of opinions was already slightly noticeable in the writings of Rolle of Hampole. It meets us fully in *Piers Plowman*. In fact, the contradictions between the several references to astrology in the poem have been employed as evidence for

held the place which astrology occupied in the beliefs of the more learned. The fact that the *Handlyng Synne*, which in this connection deals severely with fatalistic superstitions, does not mention astrology, might be taken as added proof that the latter had not penetrated to the common people of England in the early fourteenth century (the *Handlyng Synne* was written about 1303).

[1] *Polychronicon* 3. 27 (ed., with Trevisa's translation, by Lumby, Rolls Ser., 3. 401).

its multiple authorship.[1] To determine the attitude toward astrology of the author of *Piers Plowman,* two passages are of particular importance. One of these is found only in the earlier two versions. In a speech of Dame Study the poet is warned not to meddle with sorcery and magic, and the alchemy taught by Albertus.[2] Astronomy is named among the list of evil practices, alongside of geometry and geomancy:

> Ac astronomye is an harde thynge and yvel forto knowe,
> Geometrie and geomesye is gynful of speche;
> Whoso thenketh werche with the two thryveth ful late.
> For sorcerye is the sovereyne boke that to the science longeth.

The 'astronomy' condemned by the poet, judged by the company it keeps, can not have been of a very high order. It is an astrology of quite a nobler kind that is referred to by the author of the last of the three versions, in a later passus of the poem.[3] The influence of the stars upon man at birth is here taken for granted. In illustrating the difference between learning (*clergie*) and common sense (*kynde witt*), the poet says:

> Clergie cometh bote of siht, and kynde witt of sterres,
> As to be bore other bygete in such constellacion
> That wit wexeth ther of and other wyrdes bothe,
> *Vultus huius sæculi sunt subiecti vultibus cælestibus.*[4]

The fact that in the third version the earlier reference to astronomy as a magic art is omitted may suggest that the poet—whether the same as the one who wrote the earlier version or a different one—thought the condemnation too severe. It may be, too, that the general enthusiastic inter-

---

[1] This has been done by Professor Manly (*Mod. Phil.* 7. 126).

[2] Version A 11. 152 ff. (*EETS.* 28. 129); Version B 10. 207 (*EETS.* 38. 153).

[3] Version C 15. 28 ff. (*EETS.* 54. 248).

[4] In Version B, the contrast between *clergie* and *kynde wit* is given quite differently (12. 69-70: *EETS.* 38. 196):

Of *quod scimus* cometh clergye and connynge of hevene,
And of *quod vidimus* cometh kynde witt; of siȝte of dyverse peple.

est shown in astrology at the turn of the century by men like Gower and Chaucer reacted upon the author of *Piers Plowman* so as to cause him to change his views. The denunciation of the mathematical sciences in the former of the two passages is vague at best, and may imply simply a general hostility to sorcery and magic. Even if the lines had been retained in the last version, or if both had been written at the same time, the contradiction between the two would have been no greater than that found in the works of Dante and many another mediæval writer.[1]

The discussion of divination, found in the fourth book of Barbour's *Bruce,* presents an attitude toward astrology somewhat similar to that of *Piers Plowman,* although in the *Bruce* the hostile point of view is that of a rationalist, rather than that of a conservative ecclesiastic. Barbour introduces the subject in connection with a prophecy made by an old woman to the Scottish king, promising him ultimate success in his fight against the British. The fact that the prediction actually came true puzzles Barbour, and, by way of comment on the general problem of prophecy, he enters upon a lengthy excursus on astrology and necromancy. The latter, of course, he denounces as a wicked art, although he admits that demons can foretell the future.[2]

---

[1] Even in the earlier two versions, astrology is in part accepted. All three texts contain a reference to Saturn as a prognosticator of famine and flood (A 7. 311; B 6. 327; C 9. 348); and in Versions B and C (B 15. 352-64; C 18. 94-106) it is stated that shipmen and shepherds formerly predicted weather by the stars, and that the present failure of their predictions is a sign of degenerate times. Cf. also C 10. 107-8; A 10. 142. Professor Tatlock (*The Scene of the Franklin's Tale Visited,* p. 29) has already suggested that the contradictions in *Piers Plowman* are not so real as they at first sight appear.

[2] *Bruce* 748-74 (*EETS. ES.* 51. 90). Earlier in the fourth book (216 ff.), in relating the death of King Edward, Barbour cites a legend to the effect that the English monarch himself had a demon as a familiar, who, by means of an ambiguous prediction, had

A pretended science like astrology, on the other hand, he terms not only impious, but impossible. The *Bruce,* in truth—almost alone in Middle English—expresses, in addition to a distrust of astrology on religious grounds, a contempt for it as a mere fraud:

> For thouch a man his liff haly
> Studeit swa in astrology
> That on the sternis his hed he brak,
> Wis men sais he suld nocht mak,
> His lifetime, certayne domys thre.[1]

This is, however, as far as Barbour ventures in his criticism. Indeed his conscious avoidance of dogmatic assertion,[2] and his subsequent marvel at the fact that the old woman's prophecy regarding the king was successful, make it appear that he was not very sure of his scepticism. And

tricked the king into a belief that he should die at Jerusalem. Barbour calls the king a fool for trusting to even a friend's prophecy. Demons, he says, know the future, but are eager to use this gift to deceive those who consult them.

[1] *Ibid.* 709 ff. It seems that Barbour was led into the discussion, in the first place, by a genuine wonder concerning the possibility of foreseeing the future. He is evidently not at all sure that such things are impossible, though he cannot understand how a prophet can be relied on, except when he is directly aided by God.

> As it wes wonderfull, perfay,
> How ony mon throu steris may
> Know the thingis that ar to cum
> Determinably, all or sum,
> Bot gif that he enspirit war
> Of him, that all thing evirmar
> Seis in his presciens,
> As it war ay in his presens:
> As David wes and Jeromy,
> Samuell, Joell, and Ysay.

(*Ibid.* 674-83: *EETS. ES.* 55. 100. 'Determinably' probably translates the *per. certitudinem* of the scholastic theologians).

[2] *Ibid.* 674: 'As it wes wounderfull, perfay'; and 706: 'Bot me think it war gret mastry.'

Barbour was too well informed on the subject of astrology itself to attack more than the extreme manifestations of astrological divination. His maximum claim is, after all, that the astrologer cannot predict what will befall in particular cases. He admits that the 'constellations' can incline a man to good or ill, and that the astrologer can determine a man's natural disposition.[1] With regard to such general prognostications, Barbour merely makes the familiar reservation that man's will remains free even here to conquer his evil tendencies, if he so desires. He cites Aristotle as a notable example of a strong man who overcame his inclinations toward lying and covetousness. He therefore concludes, in view of so manifest a proof of man's power to shape his own destiny, that divination by the stars is 'na certane thing.'[2]

It may be stated as a general principle that the enthusiasm for astrology shown by mediæval writers varies in direct proportion to their knowledge of the subject. While many a popular religious writer might hold off from astrology as a thing in itself evil, no such general distrust is noticeable on the part of the more learned. At the opposite pole, in fact, from the attitude of Richard Rolle, was that of the great English theologian of the fourteenth century, Bradwardine. The latter's *De Causa Dei,* although written in Latin, became widely known, and its discussion of predestination and free will cannot well be overlooked in dealing with astrology in the England of the fourteenth century.[3]

[1] *Ibid.* 706-8, 716-28.

[2] *Ibid.* 746. The reference to Aristotle (736-42) is curious. The example of a man conquering his evil nature, usually cited in the literature of the fourteenth century, was that of Hippocrates (see below, p. 126).

[3] The importance in the theological disputes of the fourteenth century of the problem concerning free will, and the reflections of this dispute in Middle English literature, are noted by C. F. Brown, in *The Author of The Pearl, considered in the Light of his*

As an indication of the view regarding the subject of astrology current at Oxford, Bradwardine's treatment of the subject is in itself valuable.

Bradwardine's orthodoxy on the question of astrology is irreproachable. Inasmuch as the purpose of his chief work was a defense of the Augustinian doctrine of predestination, any rival theory of determinism found in him a stout opponent.[1] Harking back to the quarrel between the early Church and the *mathematici*, he rehearses the historic condemnation of the ancient readers of horoscopes, by the aid of plentiful quotations from Ambrose, Augustine, and Gregory.[2] The question of astrological fatalism once thoroughly disposed of, however, Bradwardine shifts from the attack to the defense. He makes no objections to the science of his own day, accepting in full the moderate astrology of Ptolemy and the scholastic theologians. Even into his exposition of the patristic doctrine he inserts a caveat to the effect that, when the astrologer indicates merely tendencies and motives, his art is legitimate.[3] The action of the stars upon man's lower nature is explained according to the familiar reasonings of Thomas Aquinas.[4] The

Theological Opinions (Pub. Mod. Lang. Assoc. 19. 115 ff.). Bradwardine is discussed at some length (pp. 128-34).

[1] Bradwardine sharply distinguishes a *necessitatio per causam superiorem* and a *necessitatio per causas inferiores.* He subjects the human will to the first, but defends its freedom over against the second. The rule of the stars would, of course, fall under the latter category; cf. S. Hahn, *Thomas Bradwardinus und seine Lehre von der Menschlichen Willensfreiheit* (Münster, 1905: Bäumker's *Beiträge,* Vol. 5).

[2] *De Causa Dei* (ed. Savile, 1618), p. 265.

[3] *Ibid.:* 'Si tamen fatum siderum nequaquam necessitatem, sed quandam dispositionem, et inclinationem in hominibus ad quosdam actus importet, non videtur penitus abnegandum.'

[4] *Ibid.,* p. 466: 'Pro iudiciis autem astrologorum, phisiognomonicorum, et cæterorum similium; advertendum quod stellæ et virtutes cœlestes multum disponunt, et vehementer inclinant corpus humanum

precepts of a 'sane astrology' are themselves made to serve against the doctrines of fatalism. It is our duty, says Bradwardine, to study the natural dispositions which have been implanted in us by the heavens, and to foster our good traits, so that they may in time conquer the bad. Bradwardine draws upon Ptolemy's *Centiloquium* for the advice that the wise man, like the shrewd husbandman, will supplement the aid given by the stars, and that by looking into the future he will fortify himself against an inevitable evil.[1] As an example of will-power conquering an evil disposition, Bradwardine relates a story from personal experience. He once met a rich merchant, he says, who confessed that the ascendant at his birth was in the first 'face' of Aries—a constellation which normally would have predisposed him to a life of homosexual lust. Bradwardine, on expressing his surprise that the man was instead a respectable merchant, learned that the latter had indeed been compelled to struggle against his inborn passions ever since he was a boy.[2] Another instance of a similar kind Bradwardine borrows from the *Secretum Secretorum,* a work supposed to have been written by Aristotle. According to the *Secretum,* students of the Greek physician Hippocrates once took a picture of their master to a famous teacher of physiognomy, only to be told

ad aliqua convenientia prosequenda, et contraria fugienda; et haec dispositio est virtus seu vitium naturale, de qua multi philosophi naturales, morales, et astrologi sæpe tractant'; cf. pp. 450 ff.

[1] *Ibid.,* p. 467: 'Nam sicut secundum Ptolomæum in Centilogio verbo 8: "Anima sapiens adiuvat opus stellarum, quemadmodum seminator fortitudines naturales"; sic secundum eundem supra eiusdem verbo 5: "Astrologus optimus multum malum prohibere poterit, quod secundum stellas venturum est, cum eius naturam præsciverit": sic enim præmuniet eum cui malum futurum est, ut possit aliquid pati, sicut et testantur experimenta superius recitata.' These same aphorisms of the *Centiloquium* and several others are used in a slightly different connection on p. 450.

[2] *Ibid.,* p. 450.

that it was the face of a deceiver and a wanton. Hippocrates corroborated the findings of the physiognomist, and informed his pupils that it was only through his power of will that he had been enabled to attain to a virtuous character.[1]

Bradwardine, in effect, although seriously opposed to astrology as a fatalistic philosophy, was an enthusiastic supporter of the legitimate science. In concluding his discussion of astrology in the *De Causa Dei,* he strongly advises all theologians to study mathematics and astronomy.[2] Astrology, inasmuch as it is the science of celestial things, is nearest to the science of God. Bradwardine finds proof in the Bible that the observance of heavenly signs is according to the will of God. The general utility of astrology is finally placed beyond doubt by additional citations from Aristotle's *Secretum Secretorum* and the Church Fathers.[3]

In the writings of Wyclif, a conclusion is reached regarding the astronomical sciences which is directly

----

[1] *Ibid.,* p. 451 ; cf. *Three Prose Versions of the Secreta Secretorum* (ed. Steele, *EETS.* 74. 113, 216). The poet Deschamps mentions Hippocrates in the course of a glorification of free will; cf. *La Fiction du Lyon* 1156 ff. (*Oeuvres Complètes,* Paris, 1882, 8. 283). It may be that Barbour, when he mentioned Aristotle as a man who had overcome his natural inclinations (see above, p. 124), had in mind this passage in the *Secretum,* and merely confused names.

[2] *De Causa Dei,* p. 467: 'Quod insuper multum deceret, et plurimum expediret theologos et perfectos Catholicos astrologiam et alias tales scientias non nescire.' Bradwardine was famous as a mathematician; cf. Cantor, *Vorlesungen über Gesch. der Mathematik* (Leipzig, 1900) 2. 113; Curtze, in *Zeitschr. für Mathematik und Physik* 13, Supplem. 81 ; Savile's introduction to the *De Causa Dei.*

[3] *De Causa Dei,* pp. 468, 469. Some of the Biblical quotations are already familiar; cf., for example, Gen. 1. 14. Others are very curious. Bradwardine interprets Matth. 16. 1 ('Ye know how to discern the face of the heaven; but ye cannot discern the signs of the times'; cf. Luke 12. 54) as implying that Christ approved of general astrological predictions.

opposed to that of Bradwardine. Wyclif's negative attitude was not so much one of hostility to astrology itself, as one of indifference to science as a whole. To the English reformer, as to the Fathers of the early Church, an interest in astronomy seemed trivial compared with the eternal issues for which he felt that he was battling. He already exhibits that literal interpretation of the Scriptures which found in the Bible an all-sufficient guide in matters secular as well as religious, and which proved in later centuries to be embarrassing to modern science.[1]

Wyclif did not formulate his conservative views on astrology at the outset of his career; nor were they founded upon ignorance of the contemporary teachings on the subject. There is evidence in his writings that he was well acquainted with the current astrological text-books; in his earlier works he seems even to have subscribed to astrological theory. There is extant a short treatise of his on comets, in which Aristotle, Averroes, Haly, and other Arabian masters are freely cited.[2] Again, in a curious passage of the *De Ente Prædicamentali,* which attempts to give a phonological explanation of onomatopœia, the influence of celestial bodies is tacitly taken for granted.[3] In

[1] Wyclif has little use for any secular studies whatsoever. Even law, grammar, and logic are to be shunned, because they are employed for private gain (*Polemical Works,* ed. Buddensieg, London, 1883, 1. 221). In his *De Veritate Sacræ Scripturæ* (ed. Buddensieg, 1906, 2. 164), he exhorts priests not to spend their time in worldly studies: 'Si igitur sciencie seculares sint postponende, quia non directe ducunt ad pietatem, que est cultus Dei, quanto magis artes contenciose et lucrative, que inducunt cultum seculi et faciunt theologiam contempni!' (cf. also *ibid.* 1. 22; and below, p. 130).

[2] *De Ente Prædicamentali,* Quæstio XII (ed. Beer, 1891, p. 297): 'Utrum cometa sit de natura celi vel elementari.' The treatise itself, which is a characteristic scholastic disputation, is unintelligible to me.

[3] *Ibid.,* p. 17. Wyclif refers to celestial influence in several other works, but his language is frequently so cryptic that it refuses to

still another instance, however, where the power exercised by the stars serves to illustrate the relation between God's foreknowledge and man's free will, Wyclif already safeguards himself by stating that astrology is introduced merely by way of example.[1]

Wyclif's mature judgment concerning astrology was distinctly unfavorable. He inveighs against it in his sermons, in his English tractates, and especially in the *Trialogus*, the treatise which he wrote at the close of his life, and which might be called his 'summa theologiae.' In all these discussions, he emphasizes the futility of astrology. He accuses the friars of practising sorcery,[2] and of studying 'veyn sophistree and astronomye' instead of the Bible.[3] Wyclif would banish, apparently, all astrology and astronomy from the schools, and substitute the pure Word of God. In one of his Latin sermons, he asserts that in the verse of the New Testament, *Erunt signa in sole et luna,* is contained whatever of truth can be found in Ptolemy's *Quadripartitum,* or in any other astronomical text-book.[4] Wyclif even joins to this religious conservatism the scep-

yield clear sense. Thus in his *De Blasphemia* (ed. Dziewicki, 1893, p. 62), it is apparently a conjunction of several untoward planets that is taken as a sign of dissension in the Christian Church. In a sermon on Luke 12. 25 ('Erunt signa in sole et luna et stellis'), the mutual dependence of earth and heaven is quite clearly accepted (*Sermones,* ed. Loserth, 1887, 1. 9).

[1] 'Quod ponatur gracia exempli' (*De Ente* 2. 7: ed. Dziewicki 1909, p. 189). Wyclif is trying to answer the question whether Peter had been free not to deny his Lord—a thing predicted beforehand by Christ himself.

[2] *De Apostasia,* chap. 2 (ed. Dziewicki, 1889, p. 41).

[3] *The English Works of Wyclif* (ed. Matthew, *EETS.* 74. 225).

[4] *Sermo XII* (*Sermones* 1. 84): 'Et sic intelligi potest Augustinus, dicens quod *in fertilitate scripture quelibet veritas est inclusa.* Nam in illo Luc. XXI, 25: *Erunt signa in sole et luna* intelligitur quidquid veritatis quadripartitum Ptolemei vel alia astronomia intelligit.'

ticism of the rationalist. As in the case of Augustine, the conviction that astrology was useless tempted him to attack it with scientific arguments. An entire chapter is devoted to astronomy and astrology—the two are never clearly distinguished by Wyclif—in the *Trialogus*.[1] After a not unsympathetic exposition of the doctrines of the double science, Wyclif proceeds to find fault with them. He objects, for one thing, to the Averroistic teaching that if a single star were added to the sky, the whole universe would cease moving.[2] Joshua's causing the sun to stand still, says Wyclif, would alone refute such a theory. Against judicial astrology itself he employs, among others, the patristic argument concerning twins. The astrologer at least cannot predict the future 'certitudinaliter.' There are many factors beside stellar influence which determine a child's fate—heredity, nutrition, and exercise; yet what astrologer takes account of these? It is clear that astrologers, like physicians, speak fiction as often as truth.[3] After Wyclif has again attacked astronomy proper, by pointing out that it is unable to explain even the simplest difficulties—whether, for example, angels regulate the motions of the planets—Wyclif passes judgment upon the whole science as follows[4]: 'Ex multis talibus videtur mihi, quod periculosum est nimis in somniis istius scientiæ immorari, specialiter cum fundatio illius scientiæ sit incerta, et fidelis posset longe melius in aliis exercitiis animæ occupari. Nec

---

[1] *Trialogus*, chap. 15: *De Cælo et Astris* (ed. Lechler, Oxford, 1879) pp. 123-7.

[2] *Trialogus*, p. 125. Wyclif singles out Robert Grosseteste for censure; cf., on the astronomy of Averroes, Renan, *Averroes et l'Averroisme* (Paris, 1861), p. 121.

[3] *Trialogus*, p. 126: 'Et patet, quod sicut medici sic et astrologi fingunt sæpe sententias quas ignorant; et talis fallacia est in arte alchimica et in multis similibus sophismatis fallaciter a trutannis.'

[4] *Ibid.*, p. 127.

dubium quin debemus Deo computum de omni occupatione virium et temporis hic in via.'[1]

Clearly, on the question of astrology, Wyclif belongs, with Petrarch, Groote, and Pico della Mirandola, to the ultra-conservative party. Like the Fathers of the early Church, these men saw in astrology a snare of the devil. Indifferent to science as a whole, and unable, in an increasingly secular age, to combat astrology with other than religious arguments, they did little to decrease its popularity.

[1] It may be remarked in passing that Wyclif shared the general mediæval belief regarding necromancy and magic; cf. *Polemical Works* I. 73; *De Benedicta Incarnatione* (ed. Harris, 1886), p. 140.

CHAPTER IX

ASTROLOGY IN GOWER AND CHAUCER

The literary interest in astrology, which had been on the increase in England throughout the fourteenth century, culminated in the works of Gower and Chaucer. Although references to astrology were already frequent in the romances of the fourteenth century, these still retained the signs of being foreign importations. It was only in the fifteenth century that astrological similes and embellishments became a matter of course in the literature of England.

Such innovations, one must confess, were due far more to Chaucer than to Gower. Although Gower, too, saw artistic possibilities in the new astrological learning, and made prompt use of these in his retelling of the Alexander legend,[1] he confined himself, for the most part, to a bald rehearsal of facts and theories. It is, accordingly, as a part of the long encyclopædia of natural science which he inserted into his *Confessio Amantis,* and in certain didactic passages of the *Vox Clamantis* and the *Mirour de l'Omme,* that astrology figures most largely in his works. By reason of this very fact, of course, it becomes all the easier to determine Gower's personal attitude toward astrology.

Gower's sources on the subject of astrology, in so far as these are at present known, were Albumasar's *Introductorium in Astronomiam,* the Pseudo-Aristotelian *Secretum Secretorum,* Brunetto Latini's *Trésor,* and the *Speculum Astronomiæ* ascribed to Albert the Great.[2] It is largely upon Albumasar and Brunetto Latini that the *Confessio Amantis* draws for the exposition of astrology which forms

---

[1] See above, p. 105.
[2] We have seen (above, p. 74) that this was probably written by Roger Bacon.

a part of the seventh book (633-1236).[1] The passage
describes at length the astrological influences of the various
planets and constellations, naming the climates which they
severally govern, and the various human dispositions which
they produce in those born under their rule. The passage
reads, in fact, like the summary of an astrological text-
book, enlivened here and there by bits of poetic description.
Of especial significance is the definition of astronomy and
astrology with which Gower opens the account—a definition for which he was largely indebted to the *Secretum
Secretorum*.[2] Ever since the introduction of Arabian sci-

[1] Macaulay (*Complete Works of Gower*, Oxford, 1901, 3. 522,
524-6) has pointed out most of the parallels between the *Confessio*
and Latini's *Trésor*. These have been supplemented by Hamilton
in a recent article (*Some Sources of the Seventh Book of Gower's
Confessio Amantis: Mod. Phil.* 9. 341-4). Gower mentions
Albumasar by name (1239). Hamilton points out (p. 20) that his
exact indebtedness to the *Introductorium* can only be ascertained
by a study of the complete text as it is found in manuscript, instead
of the abridged text of the incunabula. A parallel between this
portion of the *Confessio* and Mandeville's *Travels* has, I believe,
never been noted. In giving the astrological characteristics of the
moon, Gower says that she rules over men who roam from place
to place, and that she consequently has dominion over England,
since the English are great travelers (*Conf. Am.* 7. 749-54):

> And as of this condicion
> The Mones disposition
> Upon the lond of Alemaigne
> Is set, and ek upon Bretaigne,
> Which nou is cleped Engelond;
> For thei travaile in every lond.

The English are similarly placed under the rule of the moon by
Mandeville (*Travels*, chap. 15: ed. Layard, London, 1895, p. 199).

[2] Hamilton (*Mod. Phil.* 9. 326 ff.) has shown that Gower employed
not only a Latin text of the *Secretum*, but also a French translation
by Jofroi de Watreford. Middle English translations of both have
been published in Steele's *Three Prose Versions of the 'Secretum
Secretorum'* (*EETS. ES.* 74). The translation from the Latin (pp.
41-118) dates from the time of Gower; that from the French of

ence, the distinction between astrology and astronomy had become hopelessly confused; William of Conches and Roger Bacon had even inverted the accepted usage. It is interesting, therefore, to find the old Isidorean definitions reappearing in Gower.[1] Probably for the first time in English, astronomy and astrology are defined according to the denotations which the words bear to-day.

The passage on astrology in the seventh book of the *Confessio Amantis* seems to indicate that Gower accepted in full the science of Albumasar. Yet he is at once hostile to astrology when it assumes the rôle of a fatalistic philosophy. He prefaces his exposition of astrological theory with some thirty lines (633-63) in which he expounds the orthodox doctrine of free will. To the assertion of the 'naturiens' that all things are governed by the stars, Gower opposes the belief in an overruling Providence:

> Bot the divin seith otherwise,
> That if men weren goode and wise
> And plesant unto the godhede,
> Thei sholden noght the sterres drede;
> For o man, if him wel befalle,
> Is more worth than ben thei alle
> Towardes him that weldeth al.
> Bot yet the lawe original,
> Which he hath set in the natures,
> Mot worchen in the creatures,
> That therof mai be non obstacle,
> Bot if it stonde upon miracle
> Thurgh preiere of som holy man.[2]

Jofroi (pp. 119-248) was made in 1422 by James Yonge. The translation from the Latin preserves the numbering of chapters found in the original.

[1] *Conf. Am.* 7. 670-84 (Macaulay 3. 251). The French version of the *Secretum* cites Isidore in a passage which emphasizes the utility of astrology in medicine (Steele, p. 195).

[2] *Conf. Am.* 7. 651-63. A very similar thought is that expressed in the *Mirour de l'Omme* 26,737-48 (Macaulay 1. 296).

This view of celestial influence as a thing which was indeed a powerful factor in human life, but which stood nevertheless under the supreme guidance of the Creator, and which the true Christian did not need to fear, is a favorite one with Gower. It finds expression in the *Mirour de l'Omme*, and is made the subject of a long chapter in the *Vox Clamantis*.[1] It is epitomized in the verse of the Latin quotation prefixed to the discussion of astronomy in the *Confessio Amantis:*

> Vir mediante Deo sapiens dominabitur astris,

a line which occurs in a variant form in the *Vox Clamantis:*

> In virtute Dei sapiens dominabitur astra,[2]

and which is freely paraphrased in the *Mirour:*

> Des elementz auci je lis
> Q'al homme se sont obeiz.[3]

This Latin phrase, found generally in the form 'Vir sapiens dominabitur astris,' has a long and curious history, which is not without interest as affording numerous parallels and contrasts with Gower's interpretation. The origin of the saying is still unknown. Attributed to Ptolemy, and even specifically to the *Almagest,* it is to be found in none of his works, nor in the collection of proverbs which was current under his name.[4] The nearest approximations to

---

[1] *Vox Clamantis* 2. 217 ff. (Macaulay 4. 90-2).
[2] *Vox Clamantis* 2. 239 (*ibid.* 4. 91).
[3] *Mirour* 27,013-4 (*ibid.* 1. 299).
[4] The collection was printed in the Venice edition (1515) of the *Almagest.* I have examined the copy in the New York Public Library. It is from this list of apothegms that Chaucer's Wife of Bath (*Wife of Bath's Prol.* 182) derives the proverb which she ascribes to Ptolemy; cf. Flügel, *Anglia* 18. 134 ff.; Boll, *Anglia* 21. 229; Hamilton, p. 344. The editor of Deschamps (*Oeuvres Complètes* 11. 148) says that after a diligent search of Ptolemy's works, he is unable to locate the quotation concerning the *vir sapiens.*

the saying are two of the precepts of the *Centiloquium*,[1] which praise the utility of astrology. 'Potest qui sciens est,' so runs one of them (No. 5), 'multos stellarum effectus avertere, quando naturam earum noverit, ac seipsum ante illorum eventum præparare.' The second (No. 8) reads: 'Sapiens anima confert cœlesti operationi, quemadmodum optimus agricola arando expurgandoque confert naturæ.'[2]

Whatever be the ultimate source of the phrase, whether it goes back to a commentary on the *Centiloquium*, or was arbitrarily ascribed to Ptolemy because of its similarity to his teachings, there can be no doubt that it became known early in its present form. We have already met it in the *Summa Theologiæ* of Thomas Aquinas,[3] who employs it in an argument against predictions *per certitudinem*: 'Nihil prohibet aliquem hominem per liberum arbitrium passionibus resistere. Unde et ipsi astrologi dicunt quod *sapiens homo dominabitur astris*, inquantum scilicet dominatur suis passionibus.' John of Saxony, a Parisian astronomer of the fourteenth century, definitely cites Ptolemy's *Almagest* as the source for the saying, and interprets it, by the aid of the similar sentiment expressed in the fifth aphorism of the *Centiloquium*, as implying that forewarned is forearmed. The good astrologer, he says, is able to prevent many an evil by knowing the future beforehand, and can fortify his client to bear an inevitable misfortune with calmness of mind.[4]   Cecco d'Ascoli, in his *Acerba*, enlarges in like

---

[1] See above, p. 51.

[2] Both of these (Nos. 5 and 8) have already been quoted above, p. 126, note. See *Claudii Ptolemæi Omnia quæ extant Opera* (ed. 1551), p. 438.

[3] See above, p. 68.

[4] The passage constitutes the opening paragraph of John of Saxony's commentary on the *Isagoge* of Alchabitius: 'Vir sapiens dominabitur astris. Dicit Ptolemeus in sapientiis Almagesti. Et potest declarari sic. Ille dominabitur astris qui effectus proventientes ex ipsis astris potest impedire vel prohibere: sed hoc potest facere ni sapiens. . . . Minor probatur auctoritate Ptolemei in quinta

manner upon the advantages of astrological learning.[1] The
Secretum Secretorum—at least the French version which
Gower knew—has a curious reference to the saying, in connection with an exposition of physiognomy and astrology.
In the Middle English translation, made from the French
by James Yonge (1422), the passage reads as follows: 'And
therfor every man, of the begynnynge of his berth, by the
vertu of the sterris wych than have rewarde to hym, is
disposid dyversely to vertues and to vices. But soth hit is,
that every wyse man have vertu and will; by which he may
kepe hym anent kynde, and vertues of steris as sayth
Bugusarus the Philosofre, in the begynnyng of the Centiloge
of Tholomewe.'[2]

In the course of time, Ptolemy's doctrine of the wise
man ruling the stars gathered about itself a whole literature.[3] It found its chief popular embodiment in Jean de

propositione Centiloquii, ubi dicit: Optimus astrologus multum
malum prohibere potest quod secundum stellas venturum est cum
eius naturam præsciverit. Sic enim præmuniet eum cui malum
venturum est ut cum venerit possit illud pati.' The copy of
Alchabitius which I have used is in the Columbia University
Library. Its full title reads: *Libellus Ysagogicus Abdilazi, id est
Servi Gloriosi Dei, qui dicitur Alchabitius, ad Magisterium Juditi-
orum Astrorum, interpretatus a Johanne Hispalensi scriptumque
in eundem a Johanne Saxonie*, Venice, 1485. This is evidently the
commentary of John of Saxony of which a short excerpt is given
by L. Delisle, in *Bibliothèque Nationale: Manuscripts Latins et
Français* (Paris, 1891) 1. 27; cf. Hamilton, p. 344.

[1] *Acerba* 2. 2 (ed. Venice, 1820, p. 6).

[2] Steele, *Three Prose Versions*, p. 216. This puzzling ascription
of authorship is not found in the Latin text, at least not in the one
published at Bonn, 1501 (copy in Harvard University Library,
fol. 18[a]).

[3] Its popularity, in fact, continued throughout the later mediæval
centuries and the Renaissance. Benvenuto da Imola quotes it in
his commentary (*Commentum*, Florence, 1887, 1. 520). In the
letters of Robert Gaguin (1425-1502), it is cited in an argument
against astrologers (ed. by Thuasne, Paris, 1903, 3. 27). The

Meun's *Roman de la Rose*. Jean de Meun does not cite
Ptolemy by name, and it seems probable that he obtained his
knowledge from a secondary source, such as the *Summa
Theologiæ* of Aquinas, with whose discussion of astrology
the corresponding passage of the *Roman de la Rose* shows
general similarities.[1] In the course of a long exposition of
stellar influence, predestination, and free will,[2] Jean de
Meun recurs several times to the wise man who braves the
power of the stars by winning the victory over his own
passions. In each case his thought resembles that of the
Summa Theologiæ. To overcome the evil influence of the
constellations, Jean de Meun declares:

> Il suffit que sages se tiennent
> Et leurs mœurs natives refrènent.[3]

Italian Ludovico Moro had the saying inscribed on a cross (Burckhardt 2. 243). It was even attributed by one writer to Virgil (*ibid.*) ;
and Villon (*Codicille* 71-3 : ed. Longnon, Paris, 1842, p. 115; cf.
Hamilton, p. 344) names Solomon as the author. The precept was
popular as a convenient argument for an orthodox astrology as
late as the close of the seventeenth century; cf. Kittredge, *The Old
Farmer and his Almanack* (Boston, 1904), p. 50.

[1] Cf. with the *Summa Theologiæ* (see above, pp. 67 ff.), in addition to the lines to be quoted shortly, Jean de Meun's assertion of
the freedom of the will (17,984: ed. Marteau, Orleans, 1879, 4. 79) :

> Mais la fatalité je nie.
> Tout ce que peut faire le ciel,
> C'est leur donner mœurs et cœur tel
> Qu'ils soient enclins à faire chose
> Qui de leur trépas soit la cause,
> Par la matière dominés
> Dont les cœurs sont esclaves nés.

Langlois (*Origines et Sources du Roman de la Rose*, Paris, 1890)
names no originals for any of the astrological passages of the poem.

[2] *Roman de la Rose* 17,575-19,480. The passages which bear particularly upon stellar influence are 17,815-8, 17,865-82 (ed. Marteau
4. 67, 71). Jean de Meun's statement that in the ordinary course
of events, the stars govern everything (18,421-50), shows some
resemblance to the lines of Gower quoted above (p. 134).

[3] *Roman* 18,000-2 (ed. Marteau 4. 79).

Again, in glorifying free will, he says:

> Ainsi peut l'homme, en sa sagesse,
> Se garder de toute faiblesse,
> Ou des vertus se détourner
> S'il se veut vers le mal tourner,
> Car de soi s'il a connaissance,
> Franc-Vouloir a tant de puissance
> Qu'il se peut toujours garantir,
> S'il peut en soi-même sentir
> Quand le péché son cœur relance,
> Et braver des cieux l'influence.
> Car qui savoir avant pourrait
> Ce que le ciel faire voudrait,
> Lui-même s'y pourrait soustraire.[1]

Apparently no mediæval writer, however, found such frequent inspiration in the doctrine that the wise man is master over the heavens as Gower's contemporary, Deschamps. He refers to the saying, and to Ptolemy as its author, at least four times in his writings.[2] A firm believer in astrology,[3] Deschamps is an equally enthusiastic

---

[1] *Ibid.* 18,491-503 (4. 109).

[2] *Chançons Royaulx* 372. 33 (ed. Queux de Saint-Hilaire and G. Raynaud, Paris, 1882, 3. 124); *Balade* 289. 14 (2. 144); *La Fiction du Lyon* 1120 (8. 281); *ibid.* 1262 (8. 284).

[3] Deschamps affords an example of the ease with which a mediæval writer could combine a firm belief in stellar influence with a religious abhorrence of it in practice, especially when it could be suspected of the taint of magic. Deschamps himself wrote a treatise against divination (*Demonstracions contre Sortilèges: op. cit.* 7. 192 ff.; cf. 11. 148), in which astrology is condemned several times. The work contains a list of great rulers who came to grief because they attempted to acquire a knowledge of the future by means of divinatory arts. The other references to astrology in Deschamps' writings, however, clearly show that he did not object to a moderate use of judicial astrology; cf. especially *L'Art de Dictier* (*op. cit.* 7. 268); *Balade* 1155 (6. 88). The editor (11.148) thinks that Deschamps wrote his treatise against divination at a time of religious fervor.

champion of free will. Again and again in his ballades, and
in his long poem, *La Fiction du Lyon,* he glorifies 'franc
vouloir.' It is not surprising, therefore, that Deschamps
also follows Thomas Aquinas in interpreting the Ptolemaic
phrase as implying the possession, on the part of the 'vir
sapiens,' not so much of mere astrological wisdom, as of
the power of will to conquer his lower nature—that part
of man which alone is subject to celestial influence.[1]

The original meaning of the Ptolemaic precept was
obviously quite different from that which is given to it in
the *Roman de la Rose* and the ballades of Deschamps. As
John of Saxony and Cecco d'Ascoli well understood, the
vir sapiens designated, in the first instance, no one but the
scientific astrologer, who could employ his superior knowledge for his own ends. With Thomas Aquinas, who was
followed by Jean de Meun and Deschamps, the phrase
acquired an ethical interpretation. The 'wise man' was
no longer the learned astronomer, but the man of character,
who had indirectly gained control over the influences of the
stars by mastering the inclinations inspired by them. Now
when we turn to Gower, we find that an even more religious
turn is given to the saying. It is not so much the man of

---

[1] One quotation (*Chançons Royaulx* 372, stanza 4: *op. cit.* 3. 124)
may suffice as an illustration:

> Mais li saige, ce nous dit Tholomée,
> Les estoilles seigneurit de ça jus.
> Resister puet, et est noble vertus,
> A leur effect, et n'en faites doubtance;
> Car puis qu'il a d'elles la congnoissance,
> Il puet fuir leur male entencion,
> Et convertir en bien leur mauveuillance
> Par Franc Vouloir, selon m'oppinion.

Another poem in which Ptolemy is mentioned begins with the line:
'L'homme est la propre cause de ses maux,' and deals with exactly
the same idea that Gower expounds at length in his *Mirour de
l'Omme* (*Mirour* 26,605-27,360).

character, as the man of prayer, who rules the stars. It is only *in virtute Dei* and *mediante Deo* that the wise man is freed from the power exercised by the heavens:

> In virtute Dei sapiens dominabitur astra,
> Totaque consequitur vis orizontis eum:
> Circulus et ciclus, omnis quoque spera suprema
> Sub pede sunt hominis quem iuvat ipse deus.[1]

Both in the *Vox Clamantis* and the *Mirour de l'Omme*, many illustrations are given where God had set aside the laws of nature in answer to a holy man's supplication. Joshua, bidding the sun stand still in the vale of Gibeon, Daniel in the lions' den, the miracle of the fiery cloud, and that of Pharaoh's destruction in the Red Sea, all go to prove, says Gower, that the elements are obedient to the God-fearing.[2]

Gower was probably not sufficiently interested in the legal side of the question to tell us just where he drew the line between a legitimate and an illegitimate judicial astrology. He nowhere refers to the usual scholastic discrimina-

---

[1] *Vox Clamantis* 2. 239-42 (ed. Macaulay 4. 91).

[2] *Vox Clamantis* 2. 238-80; *Mirour* 27,013-96 (*ibid.* 1. 299-300). Note the emphasis on prayer in the passage quoted above (p. 134) from the *Confessio Amantis*. Only the 'prayer of som holy man' (7. 663) can change the otherwise immutable influence of the heavens. It is probably the *Secretum* which induced Gower to place such emphasis upon prayer in connection with astrology. At the close of a long defense of the utility of astrology, the author of the *Secretum* says (Steele, *Three Prose Versions*, p. 65): 'Wherfore yt ys mekyl worth to knowe þingys before, ffor men mowe bettyr thole hem, and eschewe hem whenne þey knowe hem to come. Wherfore men oghte wyth byse prayers bysek þe heghe destynour, þat he by his mercy torne þe evyls þat er to come, and þat he wille oþerwyse ordeyne, and for þat men awe to praye to goddys pitee in orysouns, devociouns, prayers, fastynge, services, and almesse and oþer goode dedys, bysekand forgyfnesse of hir trespas, and be rependant of hir synnes.' The French version (Steele, pp. 196-207) has a long added chapter on the subject of prayer, in which many of Gower's own examples are used (Joshua, David, Jonah).

tion against predictions *per certitudinem.* On the subject of magic he is more explicit. In the Confessor's sermon against sorcery as a means to win illicit fruits of love, full note is taken of the fact that astrology formed an integral part of the conjurer's ritual.[1] Despite his general hostility to the occult arts, however, Gower steps beyond the limits set by orthodox doctrine in condoning the practice of magic when employed for a good purpose:

> For these craftes as I finde,
> A man mai do be weie of kinde,
> Be so it be to good entente.[2]

This emancipated view of magic, which had never been sanctioned by the Church, and which was among the tenets distinctly condemned in the important edict of Paris in 1398,[3] Gower probably owed to his source, the Latin *Speculum Astronomiæ.*[4] It was for just such a condonation of magic, it will be remembered, that Roger Bacon, the possible author of the *Speculum Astronomiæ,* very likely was condemned to imprisonment at the hands of his ecclesiastical superiors.[5]

In turning to Chaucer, it is refreshing to find the didactic and controversial attitude toward astrology replaced by that of the artist. Astrology for most mediæval poets was still too novel and dangerous a subject to be treated as a

---

[1] *Conf. Am.* 6. 1338-50 (ed. Macaulay 3. 203-4):

> He makth writinge, he makth figure,
> He makth his calculacions,
> He makth his demonstracions;
> His houres of Astronomie
> He kepeth as for that partie
> Which longeth to thinspeccion
> Of love and his affeccion (1344-50).

[2] *Conf. Am.* 6. 1303-5 (*ibid.* 3. 202).
[3] See above, p. 71.
[4] Cf. Macaulay 3. 515.
[5] See above, p. 75.

matter of course, and with an unconcern for questions of right and wrong. As is the case with any strange scientific or philosophical doctrine, astrology only gradually became so generally known and so freely accepted that a writer could allude to it without running the danger, either of being misunderstood on the part of the more ignorant, or of offending against the orthodoxy of the more intelligent, among his readers. It is just this stage in the popularization of astrology, however, which is represented in England by Chaucer.

Although Chaucer here and there pauses to comment on the subject of astrology with apparent seriousness and in his own person, his references are usually dictated by dramatic or literary propriety only. His originality in employing astrology for poetic purposes is incontestable, and is, perhaps, unrivaled in the entire realm of mediæval literature. The ingenious humor of the *Complaint of Mars*—this '*jeu d'esprit* in versified astrology'[1]—is certainly unique. The clever manipulation of astrology in the *Franklin's Tale* is equally novel. While the *Filocolo* of Boccaccio, which is the probable source of the *Franklin's Tale,* employs only the vaguest kind of Ovidian magic, Chaucer enriches his story with a large amount of the astrological learning of his own day.[2] The subtle blending

---

[1] Mather, *Chaucer's Prologue, the Knight's Tale, the Nun's Priest's Tale,* Boston, 1898, p. xxxiii. Manly (*On the Date and Interpretation of Chaucer's Complaint of Mars: Harvard Studies* 5. 107 ff.) calls the poem an 'exercise of ingenuity in the description of a supposed astronomical event in terms of human emotion.' See this article for a detailed interpretation of its astrology; cf. also H. Browne, *Notes on Chaucer's Astrology* (*Mod. Lang. Notes* 23. 54); and see Hammond, *Chaucer: A Bibliographical Manual* (New York, 1908), p. 386.

[2] The difference between the magic of the *Franklin's Tale* and that of the *Filocolo* (Boccaccio, *Opere Volgari,* ed. Moutier, Florence, 1827-34, 8. 48-60), and the significance of the astrology of Chaucer's story in giving to the poem a pagan air, is treated by

of the planet Mars with the heathen god of war in the description of the Thracian temple in the *Knight's Tale* is entirely due to Chaucer. The corresponding passages of the *Thebaid* of Statius and the *Teseide* of Boccaccio contain no hints of astrology.[1] English literature also owes to Chaucer the introduction of such astronomical periphrases as that of the familiar lines of the *Prologue* (7-8),

> the yonge sonne
> Hath in the Ram his halfe cours yronne,

a type of poetic embellishment which became a commonplace in the fifteenth century.[2]

Yet the very fact that Chaucer is first and foremost the literary artist makes it unusually difficult to ascertain his own personal views on the subject of astrology. There can be no doubt of his continued interest in the philosophical problem of free will and predestination. In view of the importance which was given to the question in the

---

Tatlock in *The Scene of the Franklin's Tale Visited*, pp. 19 ff.; cf. the same author's *Astrology and Magic in Chaucer's Franklin's Tale* (*Kittredge Anniversary Papers,* Boston, 1913, pp. 339-50). On the *Filocolo* as the source of the *Franklin's Tale,* see Rajna (*Romania* 31. 40-7; *32.* 204-67); Schofield (*Publ. Mod. Lang. Assoc.* 16. 405-49); Tatlock, *The Scene of the Franklin's Tale Visited,* pp. 55 ff.

[1] *Knight's Tale* 1117-92; cf. *Teseide* 7. 31 ff.; *Thebaid* 7. 34 ff.; Hinckley, *Notes on Chaucer* (1907), p. 84. A similar mingling of mythology with astrology is found in the lines of the *Troilus* (3. 1202-4):

> But Troilus, al hool of cares colde
> Gan thanken tho the blisful goddes sevene;
> Thus sondry peynes bringen folk to hevene.

[2] Parallels for this figurative method of indicating time may be found in Dante and Petrarch; cf. Dante's *Inf.* 11. 113, 24. 1-2; *Purg.* 1. 21, 2. 56-7, 32. 53; *Par.* 27. 68, 28. 117, 29. 2; and Petrarch's *Canzone* 135. 88 (ed. Carducci e Ferrari, Florence, 1899, p. 217); *Trionfi d'Amore* 1. 4-7 (ed. Appel, Halle, 1901, p. 178).

theological controversies of the time, this is not surprising.[1] Chaucer recurs to the subject of fate again and again in his writings, and even goes out of his way to insert references to it where these are not called for in the least by his originals.[2] Although he seems never to have quite made up his mind on the relation between foreordination and free will, the references in which astrology is particularly mentioned point to the conclusion that he favored a kind of determinism. A passage in the *Man of Law's Tale*—borrowed in part from the *De Mundi Universitate* of Bernard Silvestris—expresses an outspoken astrological fatalism, although it doubts that any science is able actually to decipher the language of the heavens:

[1] See the article by Carleton F. Brown in *Publ. Mod. Lang. Assoc.* (19. 128-34). Tatlock discusses the subject of Chaucer's interest in the question of foreordination in his article *Chaucer and Wyclif* (*Mod. Phil.* 14. 265; cf. also *Mod. Phil.* 3. 370-2).

[2] The excursus in the *Troilus* (4. 958-1078) is the most conspicuous example. This passage, obedient to the dramatic requirements of the story, argues against free choice and for absolute necessity. Professor Kittredge has remarked (*Chaucer's Pardoner: Atlantic Monthly* 72. 829) that the idea of fate expressed in this long exposition 'is subtly insistent throughout the poem—it is perhaps even the key to Cressida's character.' And Professor Carleton F. Brown adds (*Pub. Mod. Lang. Assoc.* 19. 128) that 'it may be at the same time a key to Chaucer's character.' For other discussions in Chaucer of the problem of fate, see *Nun's Priest's Tale* 414-30, 518; *Complaint of Mars* 218-26; *Troilus* 2. 621-3; 5. 1550-2, 1541-5; *Legend of Good Women* 952; *Knight's Tale* 250-1; 445-54, 2129 ff. (this last is found in Boccaccio). These references include only those which are not astrological. A passage in the *Nun's Priest's Tale* (420-3) shows that Chaucer was at least superficially acquainted with some of the names which figured in the controversies regarding free will:

> But I ne can not bulte it to the bren,
> As can the holy doctour Augustyn,
> Or Boece, or the bishop Bradwardyn.

> For in the sterres, clerer than is glas,
> Is writen, God wot, whoso coude it rede,
> The deeth of every man, withouten drede.[1]

In the *Knight's Tale,* the advice of Arcite to Palamon accepts the rule of the stars over man's destinies as an unavoidable fact, and merely counsels Stoic resignation:

> For Goddes love, tak al in pacience
> Our prisoun, for it may non other be;
> Fortune hath yeven us this adversitee.
> Som wikke aspect or disposicioun
> Of Saturne, by sum constellacioun,
> Hath yeven us this, although we hadde it sworn;
> So stood the heven whan that we were born;
> We moste endure it: this is the short and pleyn.[2]

Chaucer's frequent use of such deliberate references to 'aventure' or 'destinee' as

> Were it by aventure or destinee,
> (As, whan a thing is shapen, it shal be,)[3]

> Were it by destinee or aventure,
> Were it by influence or by nature,
> Or constellacion,[4]

is also significant. In fact, it is difficult to find anywhere in Chaucer's works an appreciable softening of this extreme fatalistic philosophy. The clearest attempt to harmonize astrological determinism with the belief in an overruling Providence occurs in a passage in which Chaucer was

[1] *Man of Law's Tale* 96-8. The lines borrowed from Bernard Silvestris (cf. above, p. 34) are found in the stanza immediately following (99-105). It is worthy of note that the suspicions regarding the possibility of reading the future in the stars are additions on the part of Chaucer (cf. 97, 104-5).

[2] *Knight's Tale* 226-33.

[3] *Ibid.* 607-9.

[4] *Merchant's Tale* 723-5; cf. *Prol.* 844; *Franklin's Tale* 780. Tatlock (*Mod. Phil.* 3. 372) points to Dante (*Inferno* 15. 46, 47; 32. 76-8) for parallels.

influenced by Dante, particularly by the lines of the *Inferno* where Fortune is pictured as an intermediary between God and man:

> But O, Fortune, executrice of wierdes,
> O influences of thise hevenes hye!
> Soth is, that, under God, ye ben our hierdes.[1]

Yet even here Chaucer gives no hint that man is free to alter the decrees of this minister of destiny.

Although it would be rash, on the basis of these citations, to call Chaucer a fatalist, and to conclude that he subscribed to the astrological determinism of Bernard Silvestris, it is certainly surprising that he nowhere presents the other side of the case. Practically every writer on the subject from Alexander Neckam to Gower, while accepting a rule of the stars over mundane affairs, had with equal insistence asserted the freedom of the human will. Even scientists, who were interested in pressing the claims of astrology to the utmost, seldom espoused fatalistic theories. After the Church doctrine on the question had been crystallized by Thomas Aquinas, it was, in effect, unsafe to launch any discussion on astrology without first pledging allegiance to the orthodox teaching. Cecco d'Ascoli had been burned at the stake for failing to satisfy the Inquisition on this very point. By the close of the fourteenth century, the subject of free will and stellar influence had gathered about itself a whole literature. Yet we find Chaucer deliberately

---

[1] *Troilus* 3. 617-9; cf. *Inferno* 7. 68-88. Chaucer in several other passages refers similarly to fortune and destiny as the servants of a higher power, though he does not again couple them with stellar influence. See *Troilus* 5. 1541-5; *Nun's Priest's Tale* 179-80; and *Knight's Tale* 805-7:

> The destinee, ministre general,
> That executeth in the world overal
> The purveyaunce, that God hath seyn biforn.

These references I owe to Professor Tatlock's article on *Chaucer and Dante* (*Mod. Phil.* 3. 371-2).

ignoring all this! That he should have lacked information on the subject seems unlikely. Ptolemy and Alchabitius, it is true, are the only prominent astrologers[1] whom he mentions by name; and the only originals that he is definitely known to have used for his statements regarding astrological fatalism are Dante and Bernard Silvestris. It is strange, too, that the long discussion of the problem of foreknowledge and predestination in the *Troilus* should have limited itself to a paraphrase of Boethius, and should have passed by entirely the more recent theories on the subject.[2] But these facts do not quite make plausible the supposition that Chaucer's failure to mention the scholastic views regarding free will was due to ignorance. The *Divina Commedia* of Dante and the *Roman de la Rose* of Jean de Meun would alone have sufficed to give him full information. Is Chaucer's emphasis upon astrological determinism, therefore, to be explained on the ground that his mature judgment decided in favor of a fatalistic philosophy? Or may it be, after all, that his interest in the problem was dictated largely by artistic considerations, and that when he had employed it for dramatic and narrative purposes, he no longer cared to 'bulte it to the bren,' nor to argue it out to a fair conclusion?

How difficult it is to generalize concerning Chaucer's attitude toward astrology from the evidence furnished by scattered passages in his tales, is plainly seen in connection with his beliefs regarding judicial astrology and astrological magic. We are, namely, able to check up these latter by means of a work in which Chaucer unquestionably speaks in his own person—his *Treatise on the Astrolabe*.

Judging from the references to astrology apart from

---

[1] I ignore the list of physicians cited in the *Prologue* (430 ff.) in connection with the Doctor.

[2] Jean de Meun, who also employs Boethius (18,015 ff.), is, in general, much more modern.

those in his *Treatise on the Astrolabe,* Chaucer subscribed
to all the doctrines of the science as it was taught in his
day. Judicial astrology, in so far at least as it undertook
to define the individual's inclinations according to the configuration of the stars at birth, is nowhere condemned. The
Wife of Bath ascribes her amorous disposition to her
horoscope:

> Myn ascendant was Taur, and Mars therinne.[1]

Hypermenestra similarly derived her beauty and her character from Venus and Jupiter,[2] and owed her death in
prison to Saturn.[3] Criseyde, lamenting her fated departure
from Troy, accuses the 'corsed constellacioun' under
which she was born.[4] The astrological system of 'elections'[5] is also taken for granted. The lusty children of
Venus are said in the *Squire's Tale* to dance when that
planet is in her exaltation.[6] Troilus speeds well in love
because Venus is in her seventh house.[7] Pandarus chooses
a moment for delivering a message to Criseyde when the
moon, the patron of travelers, is 'in good plyt.'[8] The
misfortunes of Constance in the *Man of Law's Tale* are
partly due to the fact that the voyage was undertaken under
an 'infortunat ascendant.'[9] On the subject of magic, too,
Chaucer's characters hold opinions such as one might

[1] *Wife of Bath's Prologue* 613.
[2] *Leg. of Good Women* 2584-8.
[3] *Ibid.* 2597.
[4] *Troilus* 4. 745.
[5] See above, p. 53.
[6] *Squire's Tale* 264-6; cf. 121-2, where the maker of the horse
of brass is said to have awaited the proper astrological moment.
[7] *Troilus* 2. 680-6.
[8] *Troilus* 2. 74. Palamon (*Knight's Tale* 1359) goes to the temple
of Venus in 'her hour.' Damian is successful in his love-affair,
because the heavens stood in a fortunate 'constellacion' (*Merchant's
Tale* 725-6; cf. *Franklin's Tale* 53).
[9] *Man of Law's Tale* 204.

expect of mediæval folk. The Parson denounces geomancy and divination with the usual orthodox vehemence, although he is willing to moderate his condemnation in the case of medicinal charms, if they really accomplish cures.[1] Chaucer's Franklin is likewise careful to guard himself against the possible charge that he would countenance occult practices. In commenting upon the astrological magic of the Orleans clerk he seeks shelter with the orthodox doctrines of Mother Church, although he also scoffs at such things as perhaps not to be taken quite seriously in these more enlightened days:

> swich folye,
> As in our dayes is nat worth a flye;
> For holy chirches feith in our bileve
> Ne suffreth noon illusion us to greve.[2]

There is nothing, truly, in any of these references to practical astrology that is strikingly divergent from the general tenor of enlightened opinion in the fourteenth century. Although, in the persons of the Parson and Franklin, Chaucer paid his dues to the ecclesiastical hostility toward magic, he accepts a moderate judicial astrology, and the system of 'elections,' without protest. It is, therefore, surprising, in turning to the *Treatise on the Astrolabe*, to find

---

[1] *Parson's Tale* 600-10. Images made under fortunate heavenly aspects form also a part of the Doctor's stock in trade (*Prol.* 418). The reference to 'magyke naturel' in the *Hous of Fame* (1265 ff.) is non-committal on the question of right and wrong.

[2] *Franklin's Tale* 403-6. The Franklin has just been speaking of the employment by the Orleans clerk of the twenty-eight mansions of the moon. Professor Tatlock (*Kittredge Anniversary Papers,* p. 348 ff.) has shown that these stood in bad odor with the Church. Inasmuch as they belonged to the system of *electiones* (cf. above, p. 54), they could with ease be put to illegitimate uses. The clerk can probably be accused of dabbling in the black arts on other grounds as well; see Tatlock (*op. cit.,* p. 349), and cf. Chaucer's own references to the clerk's art as 'japes and wrecchednesse' (543), illusiouns' (564), and 'supersticious cursednesse' (544).

him holding a view regarding astrology in practice that is ultra-conservative. Certain astrological doctrines, which had become an inseparable part of astronomical science, he retains even here. He espouses such notions, for instance, as the characteristics of the signs of the zodiac,[1] the correspondence between the constellations and the parts of the human body,[2] and the rule of the planets over the days and hours. The prologue informs us that the work, when completed, was to include tables of astrological houses, and of the 'dignities' of planets, and 'other useful thinges.' But all these admissions are more than offset by an outright condemnation of judicial astrology itself. This occurs in a chapter treating of the astrological 'ascendant'[3]—a thing which, as Chaucer says, is greatly observed by astrologers, 'as wel in nativitez as in questiouns and elecciouns of tymes.' After discussing ascendants in general, and the various 'aspects' which render the lord of the ascendant favorable or unfavorable, Chaucer exclaims:

Natheles, thise ben observauncez of judicial matiere and rytes of payens, in which my spirit ne hath no feith, ne no knowinge of hir *horoscopum;* for they seyn that every signe is departed in 3 evene parties by 10 degrees, and thilke porcioun they clepe a Face.

If Chaucer were to be held strictly to this statement, it would go far to nullify all the positive declarations regarding judicial astrology which can be found in any of his works. To determine the nature of the ascendant was necessary for even the simplest astrological observation. The Wife of Bath uses the very word in speaking of her horoscope, and wherever else the term occurs in Chaucer, it is employed in an astrological sense.[4] Chaucer probably

[1] *Astrolabe* 1. 21.

[2] *Ibid.*

[3] *Ibid.* 2. 4.

[4] The Doctor's Images (*Prol.* 417) were made under fortunate ascendants (cf. *Hous of Fame* 1268); see above, p. 150. The use of the word in the *Man of Law's Tale* (204) refers to the observance of the ascendant for the purpose of an 'eleccioun of tymes.'

did not intend that he should thus be put to a logical test. But the passage shows unmistakably that many of the astrological doctrines which he freely accepted in the rôle of poetic narrator, he was forced to call impious when writing in cold prose.[1] Perhaps he was particularly careful to disclaim a belief in the more doubtful portions of the science, because he was writing to 'lyte Lowys my sone.'

In any case, it is interesting to observe that all of Chaucer's criticisms of magic and astrology—in the *Franklin's Tale,* the *Parson's Tale,* and the *Treatise on the Astrolabe*—object to it on religious grounds. The statement of the Man of Law that men's wits are too dull to read the language of the stars, and the Franklin's scoff at astrology as something which might have been well enough in pagan times, but which in our day is 'nat worth a flye,' do imply a certain scepticism of the astrologer's arts. Yet the main argument is still a religious one. The astrologer's notions are called rites of pagans in the *Treatise on the Astrolabe.* Holy Church, not the sceptical scientist, is appealed to in the *Franklin's Tale* in opposition to the magician's practices. The conclusion, indeed, seems inevitable that Chaucer was still under the spell of the conservative attitude toward astrology which was characteristic of the early Middle Ages, and which in England, as we have seen, was still fully alive as late as the fourteenth century.

Any attempt, therefore, to cite Chaucer's condemnation of astrology as proof that he was of a sceptical turn of mind[2] must be viewed with suspicion. The tendency, indeed, to consider early opponents of astrology as forerunners of modern enlightenment has long fostered a misunderstanding of mediæval science. From our point of

---

[1] We have noted a similar contrast between the opinion of the artist and that of the philosopher in Cicero and Petrarch.

[2] See Lounsbury's *Chaucer* (New York, 1892) 2. 497-8.

view, of course, critics of astrology, such as Cicero, Petrarch, and Pico della Mirandola, appear emancipated in an age of gross superstitions. From the point of view of the Middle Ages, however, before the days of the Copernican astronomy, these judgments deserve in many cases to be reversed. Cicero and Sextus Empiricus opposed astrology, not because they wished to replace it with a more plausible theory of the universe, but because they happened to be followers of the New Academy, and were sceptical of all science.[1] Petrarch's attack upon astrology—though it deserves all praise for its clever satire of the Italian necromancers—consists of little more than pious arguments culled from Augustine. On its scientific side, it can not endure comparison with a defense of astrology such as that of Roger Bacon. From the point of view of tradition and ecclesiastical discipline, the champions of astrology, rather than its opponents, deserve to be called modern. The spirit that enabled Cecco d'Ascoli to face execution was far more emancipated than that which animated his inquisitors. Chaucer was a bolder sceptic when he espoused astrological fatalism than when he denounced the science of judgments as rites of pagans. Like most intelligent men of his time, Chaucer probably had his doubts regarding the ability of the professional astrologer to accomplish all that his science boasted. But he was concerned chiefly about the question whether its practice was right or whether it was wrong. This fact alone would prove that Chaucer, in his personal attitude toward astrology, was still a man of the Middle Ages.

The references to astrology in the literature of the fifteenth century are of minor interest. The poetic possibilities of astrology had been largely exhausted by Gower and Chaucer, and the writers of the following decades

[1] Cf. F. Boll, in *Sitzungsber. der Philos.-Philol. Classe der Kaiserlichen Bayerischen Akademie der Wissenschaften*, 1899, p. 103.

merely imitated their masters. In fact, the allusions to astrology in the literature of the fifteenth century are important for little more than their frequency. They indicate that the popularization of Arabian science, which had begun with Adelard of Bath, was, after three centuries, virtually completed.

The dissemination of astrological learning was aided, at the turn of the century, by such works as Trevisa's translation of the *De Proprietatibus Rerum* of Bartholomæus Anglicus,[1] and by the several vernacular versions of the *Secretum Secretorum*.[2] Astrological notions were at times still taken quite seriously. Pecock's *Repressor* cites the fact that the stars produce varieties of talents in the clergy as well as in laymen as an argument for an ecclesiastical hierarchy corresponding to that of a secular government.[3] In the *Ratis Raving,* a youth is advised to consult a master of astrology regarding his inborn abilities and inclinations.[4] Robert Henryson, the Scotch poet, still harks back to the early prejudice against astrology as a divinatory art, but his strictures are plainly meant only for that astrology which prophesies with a definite yea or nay regarding contingent actions.[5] Although Lydgate, in dealing with the stories of Amphiaraus and Medea, also indulges in a

[1] The English version was completed in 1398 (cf. Wells, p. 438). The eighth book of the encyclopædia contains an outline of astrology, and is based upon Messahala, Albumasar, and others. A convenient summary is given by Langlois, in *La Connaissance de la Nature et du Monde au Moyen Age* (Paris, 1911), pp. 142-8; see *Batman uppon Bartholome,* London, 1582, fols. 118ᵃ-41ᵇ.

[2] Besides the three prose versions printed by Steele (*EETS. ES.* 74), there is extant Lydgate and Burgh's *Secrees of Old Philosoffres* (ed. Steele, *EETS. ES.* 66).

[3] *The Repressor* (ed. Babington, Rolls Ser.), p. 450.

[4] *Ratis Raving* 1. 899 (*EETS.* 43. 51).

[5] *Orpheus and Eurydice* 571 ff. (ed. G. Smith, *Scottish Text Society,* 1908, 3. 85).

polemic against astrological divination,[1] he appears, nevertheless, to have been a firm believer in celestial influence, and to have recommended judicial astrology in practice. According to Guido delle Colonne's *Historia Destructionis Troiæ,* Medea's failure to foresee her own sad future is a sign that the art of astrology is wicked. Lydgate, on the other hand, explains Medea's discomfiture as being due to her faulty knowledge of the science, and declares it a pity that her flight was not undertaken 'in good plite of þe mone.'[2]

The passages, however, in the literature of the fifteenth century, in which it is possible to determine precisely the author's views on the question of astrology, are comparatively few. The use of astronomical and astrological embellishments was becoming a conventional literary artifice, and references to astrological matters often implied as little belief or disbelief as allusions to pagan mythology. Hardly a poet from Lydgate to Spenser failed to imitate Chaucer in the employment of astronomical periphrases in

[1] The descent of Amphiaraus into hell (*Siege of Thebes* 4047 ff.: *EETS. ES.* 108. 166 ff.) is the occasion for a sermon against idolatrous astronomy. Lydgate's orthodox comments on Medea's arts are directed, not so much to her astrology, as to her general conduct and her magic (*Troy-Book* 1. 1710 ff., 3616 ff.: *EETS. ES.* 97. 62, 119). One of Lydgate's comments on magic (*Troy-Book* 1. 9071 ff.) is of interest as affording a parallel to the attitude of Chaucer. Lydgate exhibits the same curious mingling of the Christian fear of magic as something very real, though very wrong, and the more modern sceptical view that the whole thing is humbug. After describing Circe's metamorphosis of Diomedes and his followers into birds, he adds:

> But wel I wot, þouʒ my wit be blent,
> þat rote of all was fals enchauntement.
> But of our feithe we ouʒte to defye
> Swiche apparencis schewed to þe eye,
> Whiche of þe fende is but illusioun.

[2] *Troy-Book* 1. 2929 ff. (*EETS. ES.* 97. 98); 3669 (p. 120); cf. Guido delle Colonne, *Hystoria Troiana* (Strassburg, 1489), sig. b1[a].

describing the seasons of the year.[1] Lindesay,[2] Henryson,[3] and the late romancers—the author of the Scotch *Lancelot of the Laik* is particularly characteristic[4]—exhibit an abundance of meaningless astrological learning. Lydgate veritably revels in astrological descriptions, borrowing from Chaucer such tricks as the mingling of astrology with mythology in his references to the pagan gods.[5]

As we approach the English Renaissance, the *belles-lettres* cease more and more to furnish evidence regarding what men actually thought on the subject of stellar influence. Although astrology still found champions in plenty among the learned of the sixteenth and seventeenth centuries, it was already beginning its descent in the intellectual scale, and was becoming the monopoly of the maker of almanacs. In polite literature, at any rate, the question of stellar influence was seldom seriously debated. For Shakespeare and the other Elizabethan dramatists, astrology was principally a convenient source for figures of speech.

[1] See *Kingis Quair*, stanza 1 (ed. Lawson, 1910, p. 2); *Flower and the Leaf* 1 ff. (*Chaucerian and other Pieces*, ed. Skeat, Oxford, 1897, p. 361); Henryson, *Testament of Cresseid* 5 ff. (ed. G. Smith 3. 3); Lydgate, *Temple of Glass* 4 ff. (ed. Schick, *EETS. ES.* 60. 1); *Saying of the Nightingale* 1 ff. (MacCracken, *Minor Poems: EETS. ES.* 107. 221); Lindesay, *Testament of the Papyngo* 122-35 (*EETS.* 19. 227); *Lancelot of the Laik* 2471 (*EETS.* 6. 73); cf. Schick (p. cxxii) for further references.

[2] Lindesay, *Prolog to the Buke of the Monarche* 153 ff. (*EETS.* 11. 6); *Third Buke of the Monarche* 3582 ff. (pp. 117-8); *Dreme* 386 ff. (*EETS.* 19. 275).

[3] Henryson, *Testament of Cresseid* 148 ff. (ed. G. Smith 3. 8).

[4] *Lancelot of the Laik* 335 ff., 445 ff. (a passage reminiscent apparently of Gower; cf. *Conf. Am.* 7. 1450 ff.), 517 ff. (*EETS.* 6. 11, 14, 16).

[5] Examples can be found in abundance in the *Temple of Glass* (326, 328, 449, 715, 718, 835, 885, 1097, 1236, 1330, 1341, 1348, 1355); cf. also *Ave Maria* 9 ff. (MacCracken, *Minor Poems: EETS. ES.* 107. 280); *Siege of Thebes* 2553 (*EETS. ES.* 108. 106).

BIBLIOGRAPHY

The main purpose of this bibliography is to give a representative list of such books and articles as deal directly with mediæval astrology. Many of these are of a general nature and have not been cited in the notes.

TEXTS

ANCIENT

FIRMICUS MATERNUS, JULIUS, Julii Firmici Materni Matheseos Libri VIII. Ediderunt W. Kroll et F. Skutsch. 2 vols. Leipzig, 1897-1913.

PTOLEMÆUS, CLAUDIUS, Claudii Ptolemæi Omnia quæ extant Opera. Edita ab Erasmo Oswaldo Schrekenfuchsio. Basel, 1551.

MEDIÆVAL

'ABDEL 'AZÎZ BEN 'OTMÂN BEN 'ALÎ (ALCHABITIUS), Libellus Ysagogicus Abdilazi, id est Servi Gloriosi Dei, qui dicitur Alchabitius, ad Magisterium Iuditiorum Astrorum, interpretatus a Johanne Hispalensi scriptumque in eundem a Johanne Saxonie. Venice, 1485. (See Hain-Copinger, No. 617.)

BONATTI, GUIDO, Decem Continens Tractatus Astronomie. Venice, 1506.

ALÎ BEN ABÎ-RIJÂL ABÛ 'L-HASAN (ALBOHAZEN HALY FILIUS ABENRAGEL), Præclarissimus Liber Completus in Judiciis Astrorum. Venice, 1485. (See Hain-Copinger, No. 8349; Walters, p. 208.)

JA'FAR BEN MUHAMMED EL-BALCHÎ ABÛ MA'SAR (ALBUMASAR), De Magnis Conjunctionibus Annorum Revolutionibus ac eorum Profectionibus. Augsburg, 1489. (See Hain-Copinger, No. 611.) Introductorium in Astronomiam Albumasaris Abalachi. Augsburg, 1489. (See Hain-Copinger, No. 612.)

CUMONT, F., Catalogus Codicum Astrologorum Græcorum. 11 vols. Brussels, 1898-1912.

HISTORY OF ASTROLOGY

ANCIENT

BOLL, F., Studien über Claudius Ptolemæus: Ein Beitrag zur Geschichte der Griechischen Philosophie und Astrologie (Jahrbücher für Philologie und Pädagogik, Supplement 21. 49-244). Leipzig, 1894.

BOUCHÉ-LECLERCQ, A., Histoire de la Divination dans l'Antiquité. 4 vols. Paris, 1879-82.

Bouché-Leclercq, A., L'Astrologie Grecque. Paris, 1899.

Riess, E., in Pauly-Wissowa's Real-Encyclopädie der Classischen Alterthumswissenschaft 2. 1802-21. Stuttgart, 1896.

Schmekel, A., Die Philosophie der Mittleren Stoa in ihrem Geschichtlichen Zusammenhange. Berlin, 1892.

GENERAL MEDIÆVAL

Boffito, G., Perché fu Condannato al Fuoco l'Astrologo Cecco d'Ascoli? (Studi e Documenti di Storia e Diritto 20. 370 ff.).

Boner, E. G., La Poesia del Cielo da Guittone al Petrarca. Messina, 1904.

Burckhardt, J., Die Kultur der Renaissance in Italien. 10th edition. Leipzig, 1908.

Dieterici, F., Die Naturanschauung und Naturphilosophie der Araber im 10. Jahrhundert. 2d edition. Leipzig, 1876.

Dieterici, F., Die Naturphilosophie der Araber im 10. Jahrhundert. Posen, 1864.

Duhem, P., Le Système du Monde: Histoire des Doctrines Cosmologiques de Platon à Copernic. 5 vols. published. Paris, 1913-7.

Gabotto, F., L'Astrologia nel Quattrocento (Rivista di Filosofia Scientifica 8. 378 ff.).

Graf, A., La Fatalità nelle Credenze del Medio Evo (Nuova Antologia. Third Series 28. 201 ff.).

Graf, A., Miti, Leggende, e Superstizioni del Medio Evo. 2 vols. Turin, 1892-3.

Hansen, J., Zauberwahn, Inquisition, und Hexenprozess im Mittelalter. Munich and Leipzig, 1900.

Langlois, Ch. V., La Connaissance de la Nature et du Monde au Moyen Age. Paris, 1911.

La Ville de Mirmont, Henri de, L'Astrologie chez les Gallo-Romains (Bibliothèque des Universités du Midi, Vol. 7). Bordeaux, 1904.

Lea, H. C., History of the Inquisition of the Middle Ages 3. 419-549. New York, 1888.

Lebeuf, J., De l'Astrologie qui avait Cours sous Charles V, et des plus Fameux Astrologues de ce Temps (Leber, J. M. C., Collection des Dissertations, Vol. 15). Paris, 1838.

Maury, A., Croyances et Légendes du Moyen Age. Paris, 1896.

Maury, A., La Magie et l'Astrologie dans l'Antiquité et au Moyen Age, ou Etude sur les Superstitions Païennes qui se sont Perpetuées jusqu'à nos Jours. 3d edition. Paris, 1864.

Meyer, C., Der Aberglaube des Mittelalters und der Nächstfolgenden Jahrhunderte. Basel, 1884.

ORR, MARY ACWORTH (MRS. JOHN EVERSHED), Dante and the Early Astronomers. London, 1914.

PICO DELLE MIRANDOLA, Joannis Pico Mirandulæ Concordiæ Comitis Disputationum adversus Astrologos Libri XII. Venice, 1498.

SOLDATI, B., La Poesia Astrologica nel Quattrocento. Florence, 1906.

SUTER, H., Die Mathematiker und Astronomen der Araber und ihre Werke (Abhandlungen zur Geschichte der Mathematik, Vol. 10). Leipzig, 1900.

THORNDIKE, L., The Place of Magic in the Intellectual History of Europe (Columbia University Dissertation). 1905.

WERNER, K., Die Kosmologie des Scholastischen Mittelalters, mit Spezieller Beziehung auf Wilhelm von Conches (Sitzungsbericht der Kaiserlichen Akademie der Wissenschaften. Philophisch-Historische Classe, Vol. 75).

WERNER, K., Die Kosmologie und Naturlehre des Roger Baco. Vienna, 1879.

WHITE, A. D., A History of the Warfare of Science with Theology in Christendom. New York, 1903.

WÜSTENFELD, F., Die Übersetzungen Arabischer Werke in das Lateinische seit dem XI. Jahrhundert (Abhandlungen der Gesellschaft der Wissenschaften zu Göttingen, Vol. 22). Göttingen, 1877.

ENGLISH

BOLL, F., in Hoops' Reallexikon der Germanischen Alterthumskunde I. 132-6. Strassburg, 1911-3.

BROWNE, W. H., Notes on Chaucer's Astrology. Modern Language Notes 23. 53-4.

EASTER, D. B., The Magic Elements in the Romans d'Aventure and the Romans Bretons. Baltimore, 1906.

FISCHER, A., Aberglaube unter den Angelsachsen. Meiningen, 1891.

FÖRSTER, M., Beiträge zur Mittelalterlichen Volkskunde (Archiv für das Studium der Neueren Sprachen 120. 43-52).

FÖRSTER, M., Die Kleinliteratur des Aberglaubens im Altenglischen (Archiv für das Studium der Neueren Sprachen 110. 346-58).

GEISSLER, O., Religion und Aberglaube in den Mittelenglischen Versromanzen. Halle, 1908.

GERHARDT, M., Der Aberglaube in der Französischen Novelle des 16. Jahrhunderts. Berlin, 1906.

GRIMM, FLORENCE M., Astronomical Lore in Chaucer (University of Nebraska Studies in Language, Literature, and Criticism, Vol. 2). Lincoln, 1919.

Rüdiger, G., Zauber und Aberglaube in den Englisch-Schottischen Volksballaden. Halle, 1907.

Schröder, R., Glaube und Aberglaube in den Altfranzösischen Dichtungen: ein Beitrag zur Kulturgeschichte des Mittelalters. Göttingen, 1886.

Steele, R., in Traill's Social England 2. 74-82; 3. 330-1. London, 1894-5.

Tatlock, J. S. P., Astrology and Magic in Chaucer's Franklin's Tale (Kittredge Anniversary Papers, pp. 339-50). Boston, 1913.

Tatlock, J. S. P., The Scene of the Franklin's Tale Visited. (Chaucer Society Publications. Second Series, Vol. 51.) London, 1914.

Zender, R., Die Magie im Englischen Drama des Elisabethanischen Zeitalters. Halle, 1907.

WORKS CITED FREQUENTLY BY SHORT TITLES

Archiv = Archiv für das Studium der Neueren Sprachen und Literaturen, ed. Herrig. Eberfeld und Iserlohn, 1846—, Braunschweig, 1849—.

Bouché-Leclercq, A., L'Astrologie Grecque. Paris, 1899.

Duhem, P., Le Système du Monde: Histoire des Doctrines Cosmologiques de Platon à Copernic. 5 vols. published. Paris, 1913-7.

EETS. = Early English Text Society. Original Series.

EETS. ES. = Early English Text Society. Extra Series.

Migne J. P., Patr. Gr. = Patrologiæ Cursus Completus. Series Græca. 166 vols. Paris, 1857-66.

Migne, J. P., Patr. Lat. = Patrologiæ Cursus Completus. Series Latina. 221 vols. Paris, 1844-65.

Wells, J. E., A Manual of the Writings in Middle English. New Haven, 1916.

INDEX

YALE STUDIES IN ENGLISH

Albert S. Cook, Editor.

XV. Essays on the Study and Use of Poetry by Plutarch and Basil the Great, translated from the Greek, with an Introduction. FREDERICK MORGAN PADELFORD, Ph.D. $0.75.

XVI. The Translations of Beowulf: A Critical Bibliography. CHAUNCEY B. TINKER, Ph.D. $0.75.

XVII. The Alchemist, by Ben Jonson, edited with Introduction, Notes, and Glossary. CHARLES M. HATHAWAY, JR., Ph.D. $2.50. Cloth, $3.00.

XVIII. The Expression of Purpose in Old English Prose. HUBERT GIBSON SHEARIN, Ph.D. $1.00.

XIX. Classical Mythology in Shakespeare. ROBERT KILBURN ROOT, Ph.D. $1.00.

XX. The Controversy between the Puritans and the Stage. ELBERT N. S. THOMPSON, Ph.D. $2.00.

XXI. The Elene of Cynewulf, translated into English Prose. LUCIUS HUDSON HOLT, Ph.D. $0.30. (Out of print.)

XXII. King Alfred's Old English Version of St. Augustine's Soliloquies, turned into Modern English. HENRY LEE HARGROVE, Ph.D. $0.75.

XXIII. The Cross in the Life and Literature of the Anglo-Saxons. WILLIAM O. STEVENS, Ph.D. $0.75.

XXIV. An Index to the Old English Glosses of the Durham Hymnarium. HARVEY W. CHAPMAN. $0.75.

XXV. Bartholomew Fair, by Ben Jonson, edited with Introduction, Notes, and Glossary. CARROLL STORRS ALDEN, Ph.D. $2.00.

XXVI. Select Translations from Scaliger's Poetics. FREDERICK M. PADELFORD, Ph.D. $0.75.

XXVII. Poetaster, by Ben Jonson, edited with Introduction, Notes, and Glossary. HERBERT S. MALLORY, Ph.D. $2.00. Cloth, $2.50.

XXVIII. The Staple of News, by Ben Jonson, edited with Introduction, Notes, and Glossary. DEWINTER, Ph.D. $2.00. Cloth, $2.50.

XXIX. The Devil is an Ass, by Ben Jonson, edited with Introduction, Notes, and Glossary. WILLIAM SAVAGE JOHNSON, Ph.D. $2.00. Cloth, $2.50.

XXX. The Language of the Northumbrian Gloss to the Gospel of St. Luke. MARGARET DUTTON KELLUM, Ph.D. $0.75. (Out of print.)

Printed in the United Kingdom
by Lightning Source UK Ltd.
111681UKS00001B/22